NINE BOATS
&
NINE KIDS

by

Jeanne St. Andre Merkel

first printing - 1984
second printing - 1985

1984
LEDGE BOOKS
Box 19
Bernard, Maine 04612

Library of Congress Cataloging in Publication Data
Merkel, Jeanne St. André, 1930-
Nine boats & nine kids.

Bibliography: p. 155
1. Boats and boating.
2. Merkel, Jeanne St. André, 1930-
3. Boatmen--Biography.
    I. Title.
    II. Title: Nine boats and nine kids.
GV775.M4   1984   797.1'092'2 (B)   84-19422

ISBN 0-931447-003 paperbound
ISBN 0-931447-01-1 hardcover

Photographs by Joseph and Jeanne Merkel
Plan of Joel White's LADY JEANNE Redrawn by Spencer Lincoln
        Courtesy of WOODENBOAT MAGAZINE
Cover Design by Wade Hancock
Printed by Furbush-Roberts Printing Co., Bangor, Maine

Major portions of this book appeared originally in OFFSHORE and
WOODENBOAT magazines.

CONTENTS

I

STEELCRAFT SEDAN
1947 26'

"HOLIDAY"
Power: Chrysler Crown 125 h.p. gas

In the spring of 1984 after thirty years of living and dreaming boats we sold our beautiful LADY JEANNE, ninth in a line of lovely boats that goes back to 1954. As I signed the papers that transferred title to her new owner my mind went back across the years. Nine power boats, ranging in size from 24 to 54 feet. Six of them factory built production boats, three of them custom built to our order. Except for the first all have been built of wood.

Those wonderful boats! They have absconded with much of our wealth, exacted endless labor, filled our nights and days with scheming and dreaming and provided us with joys, sorrows and memories never experienced by shorebound folk.

During these same years while so many of our resources have been allocated to boating, we have also borne and raised nine children: five girls and four boys. Sometimes it seems as though the personalities of the nine boats we have owned have been as varied as the personalities of the nine children: their nurturance has been almost as demanding. The anticipation of each addition to our family, interspersed over the years with the struggles to find and acquire each boat, the work involved in making them truly sea-worthy, and the cruises: river, sound and coastal, have filled our lives to overflowing.

We began with harbor-hopping from our home in Glen Cove, New York. Next, we explored the rivers of Connecticut. Then we graduated to the Hudson and Mohawk Rivers of New York and Lake Champlain in Vermont and the Richelieu River in Canada. Finally we ranged out to Shelter and Fishers Islands, and growing bolder, eventually cruised to the rocky coast of Maine. In 1979 we decided to retire in the shadow of Mount Desert's beautiful mountains.

Our children, our boats and our travels, combined with four major relocations made in an effort to cruise in clean water, plus the establishment and operation of our family business, a day care center which since 1966 has cared for over two thousand children, have provided us with an education and history hard to match for excitement and hard work!

The children part of our life adventure really started fifty years ago when I was four and already dreaming of the day when I would have a baby of my own ... lots of babies, as a matter of fact. I was the oldest of six children and my mother was my idol. As a teenager I always warned my dates of my ambition ... at least six children including a set of twins; I had twin aunts so this was a valid dream. I still believe that my husband was a brave man to take me on. We were married on Memorial Day in 1948 and began our marriage with an adventure that was to set the pattern of our life together: DO IT! DON'T JUST DREAM! We took a three month honeymoon trip to California driving out on Route 66, working for two months in San Francisco and returning through Canada in time for Joe to begin college in September. When we got back to New York we had five dollars in our pockets. I went to work and Joe hit the books but after a year he realized college was not for him. Postwar construction was booming on Long Island and he went to work. Joyfully we started our family.

The boat part started innocently enough, as such things do, with an invitation to spend a day on a friend's boat. Little did we realize on that fall day in 1953 as we stepped aboard George Slonczewski's 26' Steelcraft with our four little kids (Michele, 4, Joey, 2½, Renee, 1½, and Jeff, 6 months) that we were about to be HOOKED! There's no other way to describe the disease; once nature lovers experience life afloat, no other life seems bearable. The very next week we started haunting boat yards and following up ads ... our objective: a safe, comfortable, economical powerboat which would provide the necessities for living aboard for weekends and vacations. I already knew too well that small children needed dependable bedtimes and meals.

As I recall this true-life adventure our family has dwindled to just the two of us: old lovers who have tried to realize their dreams of a big family of beautiful children and happiness forever after on a safe, beautiful, economical little ship. Our first eight children have married and are blessing us with sweet grandchildren, thirteen born already and another due in October. Our LADY JEANNE is gone! What can ever replace that dream?

During all these years of boat owning and boat buying we have lived immersed in a frenzied, anxious, hopeful, romantic quest ... before us always the hope: maybe this time it will be PERFECT! But, perfect for what purpose and at what cost? When we started looking for our first boat we were severely limited. Every working family knows the story. In 1953 it was a few hundred down and three years to pay. Now it is several thousand

down and ten or twelve years to pay. In spite of this, we have worked ourselves up to some very good boats. We learned something from every one.

When we first started looking for a boat, Joe was working seven days a week in construction. The only days we could search were rainy days when there was no work. We soon discovered that there's no better time for boat hunting since all leaks in the topsides and cabins are immediately apparent. Dry bunks are close to the top of my boating priorities.

We had decided to try to find a Steelcraft like George's. There were quite a few of them around after the war, the prices were within our limits, and they had a lot of living room for their size.

One rainy day we drove almost to Montauk Point on a wild goose chase ... the boat we went to look at was completely unsalvagable. As always, the babies were all with us. That was before the Long Island Expressway and it had been an endless day. Tired and discouraged we drove through Huntington, scarcely aware, eager for home, when, behind a closed gas station we caught sight of a 26′ Steelcraft ... and YES, there was a *4-sale* sign!

The boat was named *HOLIDAY!* Joe called the owner and he came down and unlocked the boat. The children tried out the bunks ... there were four. I studied the galley ... I could manage with it. The dinette in the little wheelhouse folded down with some difficulty to a skimpy double bunk for Joe and me. Fortunately, we were pretty slim. The flat head six cylinder Chrysler Crown engine looked clean and the owner assured us that she ran well.

So it began. I don't remember how we raised the money: $2,600; we had a new little ranch house and lots of doctor's bills. Joe was working seven days a week trying to make ends meet, but we had caught sight of a dream and nothing could stop us. Against all reason we began the first of many banking relationships. Fortunately, Joe was a good, steady worker and the construction trades were expanding on Long Island. No bank ever lost money on us.

We had the HOLIDAY hauled to Wilkinson's Boat Yard in Bayville, New York. Spring '54 was fast approaching and there was an awesome amount of work ahead to make the boat really safe and livable. We were determined to get cruising that summer. Our friend, George, wanted us to take a cruise to the Connecticut River over the Labor Day weekend. George was still a bachelor so he usually took one or two friends on cruises, and though Joe and he were best friends Joe would never go without me and the children ... now we could all go together.

My younger brother, Dave, was asked to make the trip with George so he tried to help us get the boat ready. Many times during that spring and early summer he'd pick up the children and me and take us to the boat yard where we'd set up the playpen in the shade for Jeff and Renee and give Joey and Michele strict limits, while he and I attacked the steel bottom with scrapers and wire brushes. When Joe got home from work dinner was on the table, so he could eat and run down to the boatyard. I stayed home with the babies since we could not afford sitters, while he went off alone and

worked with drop lights and flood lights till he was ready to drop. So began the reclamation of the first boat. His modus operandi fell into a pattern that was to be repeated five times in the years ahead with every "previously owned" boat.

First: a big box for all the junk! I don't know why boat owners never throw anything away ... old parts, cans of dry paint, rusting tools, torn and outdated charts, swollen cans of food, soggy life jackets ... they all seem to be the same. If any piece of equipment was beyond restoration to some degree of shine, that would go out too. We'd just have to buy a new one!

Next, up with all the hatches and scrape out the bilges: wood and metal shavings, screws and washers, fish scales, dead shrimp and sea shells, sand and mud, even an occasional olive. Scrub with bilge soap till all old oil and grease were loosened, then allow to dry and vacuum every crevice.

Then out would come the wire cutters and a bucketful of wires that had been disconnected through the years would be cut and removed. Every electrical connection would be tested and checked, terminals scraped, fuel lines replaced, shaft alignment checked, light fixtures replaced or polished.

After that would come the Spic and Span, the Comet cleanser, the 3M scrubbers and buckets of water. Any spots of rust or rot would be dug out, treated, re-filled, sanded and primed. Finally, a beautiful, tasteful paint job with the best yacht paints. When Joe finished with a boat it was a thing of beauty!

I would re-cover the cushions and make curtains, line the galley drawers and assemble the necessary tools of my trade: dishes, pots, linens, pillows, blankets, sleeping bags, first-aid, grooming and cleaning equipment and supplies.

Come to think of it, my husband's attention to detail was probably the only reason I could even consider taking our four beautiful babies to sea. The most important requisite for any mother of such children is a good captain ... and that we have always had!

Finally, HOLIDAY was ready. It was already into July when we launched and brought the boat to a rented mooring off Morgan's Beach in Glen Cove. The engine started without too much trouble and our boating life began.

As I said, Joe worked seven days a week, so the only time we could use the boat was in the evenings and on rainy days. Even that couldn't dampen our eagerness. Every evening I had dinner ready in the cooler, the children bathed and their pajamas and sweat shirts packed. We would be sitting on the stoop, watching for Joe; as soon as he pulled into the driveway we'd pile in the car and head for the shore, life jacket the kids, load the dinghy and row out to the boat.

The kids and I would row around in the dinghy while Joe went aboard. He would open the engine hatch and check the fuel lines, then start the engine. Only after making sure everything was safe would he help us aboard. We have never taken gas engines for granted; better safe than sorry!

Our evenings aboard fell into a pattern. On clear evenings we'd take the boat out past the breakwater and head toward Rye Beach; the lights of the rides would provide a target and as night deepened we often enjoyed the

fireworks. Halfway across the sound we'd turn around and head back toward the light on our breakwater. On the way back I'd give the children their dinner, then get them into their pajamas. As they wound down I tucked them into bed. When we got back to the mooring Joe and I would have dinner, lingering over our coffee and enjoying the beautiful night sky, watching the moon rise or wane while our little ones slept.

Along about ten o'clock I'd slip them into their life jackets, then I'd climb into the dinghy and Joe would hand them down to me ... two oldest first in the bow, two youngest on either side of me ... balance the boat ... then he'd climb down ... careful ... and row us ashore ... a ten minute ride home, tuck the kids in again, then take our baths ... 5:30 A.M. came all too soon.

After about a month of that routine Joe told his boss that he would not work on Sunday afternoons any more. We started to extend our cruises westward to Port Washington and Manhasset, eastward to Cold Spring Harbor and Huntington. We learned to read our charts and time our runs from buoy to buoy, eyes glued to compass. Fair weather sailors, we stayed on our mooring when it was rough or foggy, but we gradually gained confidence in our boat and in our ability to handle her. By the time Labor Day weekend arrived we were ready to enjoy our first long weekend trip.

Renee, Michele, Joey and Jeff. Ready for the first cruise.

George in his boat with my brother, Dave, and another friend, Bucky, met us in Glen Cove after work on Friday. I can still remember the excitement of that first rendezvous; we were off to a great adventure. We planned to spend the night in Fairchild Basin just east of Cold Spring Harbor, not quite ten nautical miles from our mooring. Our failure to take account of the early September time of sunset brought us to our destination just a few minutes after darkness had settled over the water. The unmarked entrance to the "sand hole," never really easy to find even in daylight, was impossible for us unskilled seamen in the dark. We missed it entirely and though we were barely moving we drove the boat hard aground on the sandy spit to the east of the entrance. We warned George just in time and Joe leapt ashore with a flashlight and guided the other boat into the mooring area where they were soon anchored and ready to help us.

The tide was almost ready to turn so we anchored seaward and waited. Bucky gamely donned swim trunks and checked our prop which needed some straightening. Careful examination showed no leaks or damage. After an hour or so the tide freed us and we followed George's light into the mooring, rafted up and fed everyone. The children settled down for their first full night aboard and we followed soon after. What a beginning!

Dawn came all too soon and was signaled by a big splash and a yell. Bucky, out for his morning dip, a sound we were to hear every morning that he cruised with us. (Bucky is Graham Buchwald, now a Long Island Lighting Co. executive.) With the children still snug in their bunks we crept into the sound, found the bell off Lloyds Neck and 11B off Eaton's Neck and then took an 87° course to Stratford Shoal Horn, fourteen miles away. Our next heading was 55° which took us the thirteen miles to the #1 Bell off of New Haven. Following the coast we passed outside the Thimbles, inside Falkner Island, then east to the Saybrook breakwater.

As we passed behind that breakwater I breathed a mighty sigh of relief ... feeling almost as though an ocean had been crossed rather than Long Island Sound. We made our way up the Connecticut River, through the open bascule bridge and under the high fixed bridge; creeping behind Calves Island we dropped anchor for the day. After a hearty late lunch, Joe and all the "uncles" took Michele and Joey in tow and in two dinghies they explored the harbor and island while Renee and Jeff napped and I enjoyed what was left of the sun.

That evening after supper when all the children were settled for the night George brought out the playing cards, his signal for a few rubbers of bridge, and we began a tradition that was to see us through many rainy days and quiet evenings. As our family increased and matured we taught all of them to play bridge; it's amazing how quickly even six year olds can learn. None of us ever became really expert but hundreds of lively evenings grew out of that early learning; a couple of funny prizes and a few "special" refreshments and we always had a party. Once grown, when they came as adults to spend a night on our boat they always requested a bridge game. I hope they never forget those happy times. I never shall.

The next morning we were up early to cruise the river, past Essex and between green and rolling hills, we followed the twisting channel for a couple of hours, then retraced our course to Hamburg Cove. We ate, swam and rowed around the moored and anchored boats. Though we've dropped our hook in many beautiful coves since, Hamburg Cove was the first, and will always have a special place in our memories.

The children enjoyed watching all the different boats and waving at the friendly strangers. Nowhere else in the world are people as friendly as on the water and everywhere we went people took pleasure in the sight of our happy little crew. We all saved crusts to feed the ducks and seagulls, and sometimes even whole families of swans. The cockpit was high sided, like a big play pen, and the children all learned right from day one that they couldn't climb up on chairs and hang over the edge ... it just was NOT ALLOWED!

The self-discipline Joe and I developed to assure the children's safety on the water was probably the best reward; it made it possible for us to have the big family of our dreams and in spite of all the work really enjoy every one of our children.

"HOLIDAY" on the Champlain Canal
l to r: Jeanne, Michele, Renee, Jeff and Joey

The last morning of our long weekend dawned cold and breezy; overnight, autumn had arrived. Joe was due back at work the next day, so, in spite of a pretty nasty chop, and because of George's encouragement, even insistence, we left the safety of the river and took a course for the bell at the western end of the long sand shoal, then, quartering the considerable sea, we followed George diagonally across the middle of the Sound.

That day we decided that if we got home alive future cruises in the Steelcraft would be more carefully planned. Crossing Long Island Sound would be limited to mid-summer. Spring and fall cruises would utilize less turbulent bodies of water. In short, we had a very rough day! Had our boat been less sound or our engine failed I might not be writing about it, but we made it home, tired and drained, but somewhat proud as well.

We continued to take short cruises on pleasant fall Sundays, but the shorter days and often choppy seas at our exposed mooring made evening outings too risky. We hauled and stored the boat in October. We were bereft without it; in one short season it had monopolized our lives.

1955

A winter spent studying charts and boating magazines followed our first summer of boat ownership. Long before the snow melted we had determined to head for Lake Champlain via the Hudson River and the Champlain Canal. With the kids still so small it seemed the better part of wisdom to cruise in more protected waters and stay in sight of land.

Joe told his boss that he was going to take a two-week vacation as soon as school was out and that he would not work weekends during the summer. His boss was a hard working contractor to whom the most important thing was the JOB, while we had finally realized that there was definitely more to life. This would be our first vacation since our honeymoon all of seven years before.

Because Joe had done such a good job the first year and left the boat so clean at haulout, spring painting and commissioning were accomplished in time for us to plan a Memorial Day weekend cruise around Manhattan Island. We felt that would be a helpful preparation for our vacation trip to Lake Champlain, since the beginning of our vacation cruise would cover the same courses.

Jeanne works on her tan while the kids watch the big ships ...
cruise around Manhattan Island. May 30, 1955.

Excitement mounted as we prepared for our first long vacation. The children were getting old enough to appreciate the history and geography of the areas we would travel; we read about and discussed the new places we would see from the water for the first time. Once again, George and my brother, Dave, and another young friend of George's made the trip with us. It was comforting to travel with another boat while our children were so young. George had several years of boating experience behind him and he taught us all he knew of safety, boat maintenance and navigation. One less enjoyable part of cruising together was George's insistence on crack of dawn starts and long, hard driving days. He couldn't wait to get going in the morning and usually roused us at 5:00 A.M. while I would have preferred to sleep as long as the children would let me (which was never very long). The days planned run was often a full twelve hours, really too long a day for all of us. Fortunately, the children did not seem to mind; we had school time, cookie time, nap time, etc., and they never tired of watching the passing show.

Our first Champlain trip began at 5:00 A.M. on a promising late June morning as we picked our way from buoy to buoy in the early mist, past Manhasset Neck's Sand Point and Great Neck's Hewlett Point. In just over an hour we rounded Throg's Neck and were in the East River with its early morning bustle. We passed Riker's Island, went around Ward's Island and into the dirty Harlem River with its dozen bridges, auto graveyards and railroad switching yards. We wakened the older children in time to enjoy the excitement, but it was a relief to ease into the Hudson River at Spuyten Duyvil Creek. After the Harlem the Hudson looked like a queen of rivers sparkling ahead of us.

Our plan for the day called for about 56 miles of the Hudson to Wappinger's Creek, where George assured us we could anchor safely for the night, out of the way of river traffic. Following the channel on the Hudson required our close attention. It was all new to us and the day beacons which marked the winding course were often hard to find.

Since the lower river, Haverstraw to Kingston, is notorious for rocky shoals off the channel accurate headings were crucial. We tried to keep a wide berth of tugs towing long strings of barges and oil tankers, deeply laden and heading north or buoyantly speeding south.

It was almost dark when we pulled into Wappinger's Creek. It seemed like a desolate, lonely spot, quiet except for an occasional train rattling across the trestle. (Old time radio buffs may remember the Saturday afternoon Grand Central Station program which began with "great trains" that "swept down the eastern bank of the Hudson River before burrowing beneath the glitter and swank of Park Avenue." Here was where they "swept by.")

We were exhausted after that long day of constant vigilance so it was early to bed for everyone ... no bridge game that evening.

In the middle of the night we were awakened by a piercing scream. Joe and I leapt out of bed and while he groped for light I went below to the children. I found Renee on the floor and picked her up to find her face covered with blood. Anyone who has children knows how much they bleed when wounded; it always looks so much worse than it is. There was a little metal lip on the door sill between the main cabin and the head compartment forward, not big enough to be perceived as a danger but, somehow in falling out of her bunk Renee managed to catch it just wrong. When we got her cleaned up, the wound was a deep but clean ¾ inch gash in her left temple. If we had been at home I'm sure I would have taken her to the emergency room for a couple of stitches, but we were miles from anything in a strange, lonely creek. Not one light showed ashore. We would just have to manage. Joe remembered from his days as a Navy Corpsman how doctors often used hour-glass shaped adhesive tape instead of stitches. While I comforted Renee, cleaned and kept pressure on her wound, Joe carefully cut adhesive to the remembered shape. Luckily, no infection complicated the healing process and there were no signs of concussion. Renee still has a very small scar as a souvenir of that trip, but probably no worse than stitches would have left.

When we got up the next morning we found the whole outside of the boat plastered with dead mosquitoes; we couldn't see out of the windshield. Joe had to wash the whole boat before we could begin the day. That was the only time in all our cruising that we experienced such an invasion. With the medical emergency of the night and the mosquito invasion of the morning Wappinger's Creek became an unforgettable stopover.

That day's run was planned to take us about ninety miles to Troy. This stretch of the river was less rocky but there were numerous mud flats and shoals to be aware of. The weather held clear and pleasant as we neared Albany, alert for river debris and avoiding the heavy commercial traffic around the port of Albany. We dropped our hooks for the night at the Troy Motor Boat and Canoe Club, eight miles above Albany and one and one half miles below the Troy Lock and Dam, otherwise known as the Federal Lock. George had anchored near this club on previous trips and looked forward to the friendly welcome from other cruising people.

Joe and George went ashore for some groceries, newspapers and ice cream for everyone. After dinner we discussed our plans for the following day. We had never gone through locks before and were somewhat apprehensive.

I understand that much work has been done on the locks since we cruised the canal; recessed vertical pipes have been installed to make securing the boats during lifting and lowering safe and easy. In those days, the sides of the locks were rough and gaping, rusting ladders on the sides had to be climbed to the top of the lock to secure lines. I can't imagine how anyone old or portly could have managed. It was very easy to do considerable damage to your boat if the crew was careless. Both of our boats were freshly painted and the source of much pride ... we had no intention of being careless.

Since George's crew consisted of three men: one to hold the ladder and two to fend off at bow and stern, it was decided that they would enter the locks first and get themselves secured and we would follow with all fenders on the starboard side and secure to them. This turned out to be a good plan which made it possible for me to watch the children without distractions. Once in a while situations arose which made it impossible for us to do this. At those times I would sit the children in the dinette with strict orders to "STAY PUT," and help Joe protect our boat during the locking. Sometimes the lock tenders would let the water in and out with great speed which caused much turbulence and made it almost impossible to hold on and keep the boat straight so it wouldn't get damaged.

The next morning we were waiting just below the Federal Lock when it opened at 8:00 A.M. This lock was designed for commercial traffic, 492 feet long, 44 feet wide, with a low water depth of 13 feet and a lift of 17 feet.

The canal consists of 11 locks; the first eight lift you up, 9, 11 and 12 let you down. There is no lock 10; it was laid out in the survey but turned out to be unnecessary. The part of the canal which contains the locks runs for about 60 miles from Waterford to Whitehall, and normally we would have easily done that many miles in one day, but as it developed we lost almost an hour for each lock: waiting for them to open on the hour, getting all the boats secured, the actual lift which took about twenty minutes, opening the gates and unfastening lines. The speed limit on the canal is 10 mph., so even more powerful boats have no advantage. We always cruised the Champlain Canal in June when it is not as busy; I understand that in July and August the traffic increases to the point where all the waiting boats can't fit in the lock and I imagine it gets uncomfortable waiting in those sheltered coves with summer sun and winged pests.

We reached Schuylerville by mid-afternoon and decided to take a break. We put up at a very friendly marina and I did some wash at the Laundromat while Joe and the uncles took the children swimming upstream. They brought cakes of soap with them and everyone had a good lathering well away from the marina. The kids thought that was a funny kind of bath ... but better than none ... and one of the advantages of cruising in fresh water. I found the long dock water hose full of warm water, so I enjoyed a shampoo in a basin at the end of our float, and rinsed the children when they returned from their swim-bath. It was a pleasant, well remembered interlude.

The next day we went as far as Fort Ticonderoga, anchored off the fort and rowed in. The spot where we came ashore turned out to be a cow pasture. A recent cruising guide describes the situation: "Landing facilities are poor and crusing craft should not approach." In those days we did not have the advantage of a very helpful cruising guide to tell us how to approach scenic and historical points of interest, so we just took the most direct route. We climbed the fence and dodging cow flops invaded the fort from an unguarded flank. We enjoyed the tiny military uniforms and the old weaponry on display at the fort. The children still remember that hilarious climb through the dung and the excitement of getting in "free." Today, I guess I would find the gate and pay like a grownup, but then I was still kid enough to enjoy putting one over on the powers that be.

One more day took us through the last lock just north of Whitehall. After that the narrow river-like channel turned to port and for the next 15 miles it wound through marshes to the southern narrows of Lake Champlain.

The strain of the locks behind us, we enjoyed the foothills of Vermont's Green Mountains to starboard and New York's Adirondacks to port. Having heard that Vermont had more cows than people the children spent tireless hours counting cows as well as swatting the numerous flies that seem to go with them.

Once we reached the lake we really had a chance to relax. We anchored in a different cove every night, depending on which way the wind was blowing. We explored the shores, had picnics and cookouts, found warm, rocky pools for bathing and swimming since the lake is mostly quite cold in June, and walked miles to little towns along the shores. We didn't try to carry too many groceries since we found it fun to visit the stores in little villages, talk to anyone who was friendly and get the children some ice cream. Shopping was an important part of each day's entertainment. The boys all had snorkeling gear and I discovered its pleasures for the first time. How I enjoyed floating effortlessly around the boat watching the schools of brightly colored fishes and the waving plants in that clean water.

The weather was mostly good; as I remember there was just one thunder storm which came up suddenly on the lake and gave us an anxious half-hour. Several nights we were awakened with a sickening realization ... the anchor was dragging! Often during the night the wind would swing completely around ... usually at about 2:00 A.M. Since we were always rafted up with George's boat whoever realized the situation first would wake the other skipper, both engines would be cranked up, George would study the chart and the wind and make a decision, we'd cast off our lines and follow him in the darkness. His anchor down and holding, we'd come alongside and secure lines, then settle down and try to get back to sleep. Since I'm one of those people who once wakened can't settle down again, I spent many nights feeling the lift and roll of the boat, listening to the night noises and watching the setting moon and the rising sun across the dark and lonely waters. Busy with my family all day, I enjoyed the night hours of thinking and dreaming ... and the time to sort things out, solve problems and store memories.

HOLIDAY. Locking through on the Champlain Canal.

When there were just four days left in our vacation we reluctantly turned homeward. On the return trip we stopped in different places than we had on the way north. This is a practice we always continued; in this way we have extended our cruising knowledge to many additional harbors. Should an emergency arise it is comforting to know that there is a familiar port in reach.

Twenty-nine years have passed, but I still recall how subdued the whole family was as we rounded Manhasset Neck and caught sight of our breakwater in Hempstead Harbor. It was all over! We would have to wait a whole year before we could do it again: live aboard and travel for two weeks. Back to the world of work and responsibility.

We were determined, however, to make the most of every weekend. I wonder now how we squeezed so much in. By covering a lot of miles each day, of course, something we seldom try to do now. Then, we wanted to see everything, go everywhere. Ah, youth!

One weekend it would be the Mystic River, then the Connecticut River again, this time to Hartford. Then once more around Manhattan Island, this time in the opposite direction. Our Chrysler Crown was a thrifty engine and gas was still cheap. Since we carried our home with us it didn't cost much to cruise. I've never known a family to really use their boat as we did.

By the time we stored the boat I was expecting our fifth child. We had already planned to return to Lake Champlain for two weeks beginning July 4, 1956. The baby was due in the middle of June. Both grandmothers became frantic! How could we take such a little baby all the way to Canada on the boat? I think they felt we were crazy.

1956

Once again Joe had the boat ready for a Memorial Day outing but with the baby due in two weeks we stayed close to home. I scrubbed up my little white bassinet and took it down to the boat; it just fit behind the helm seat without blocking the passage. We were all set. I was planning to nurse the baby, so there was no worry about strange milk.

During every pregnancy I had been troubled with varicose veins and this time they became impossibly painful and ugly. I saw a surgeon who agreed to surgically remove the worst veins while I was hospitalized to give birth. I did not want to be away from my young family twice.

By the time Marie was born on June 25th everyone was sure I had counted wrong and that our vacation plans would have to be scratched. But, no, she was only ten days late; holding out to put on ounces like a smart girl ... she weighed in at just 6 lbs. 8 ozs.; my smallest baby to date.

Two days later I had the surgery on my legs. It turned out to be more than I had bargained for. I couldn't climb stairs for almost a month and time on my feet was strictly limited. With five small children to care for I needed a full time nurse ... the only solution ... take our vacation as planned and thus have my husband on hand as needed. The older children were already becoming good little helpers, and a boat is an ideal place in which to get rested ... no stairs to climb and Daddy there to help. Marie was just ten days old when we left. Once again, George and his crew made the trip with us.

We were old hands at locking now, but with the baby to care for and my legs in constant pain I needed help. The men agreed to give me a vacation ... when we were locking one of the boys from George's boat would come aboard our boat to help Joe. The kids loved these long visits from their favorite "uncles." We also got in the habit of anchoring by ourselves so that the baby's night time stirrings would not disturb the bachelors' sleep.

Everywhere we went people said they had never seen such a tiny baby cruising. I washed diapers as soon as there were half a dozen dirty, and there was always wash strung on the back deck. Those were the good old days ... remember ... before Pampers!

We had hoped to cruise the Richelieu River all the way to Sorel, but by the time we reached Chambly Basin it was time for us to begin the return trip. The Chambly locks are manually operated by tenders who live in little French looking houses near the locks. That part of the trip had a picture book quality we all really enjoyed. Hearing all the voluble French reminded me of my childhood days when hordes of French-Canadian relatives descended for fun-filled holidays. The days we spent in Chambly Basin were the highlight of that trip. The men all bought white and blue French hats with red pompoms and the children and I practiced our limited French.

PICTURE TAKING ON THE BOW OF "HOLIDAY"
Renee, Joey, Jeanne, Jeff and Michele
The boys are wearing the Canadian hats

When we arrived home from that trip we still had a busy summer ahead of us. That spring we had decided to move further east, since Hempstead Harbor was becoming more and more polluted. It just wasn't fun swimming at dirty beaches. We had sold our house in Glen Cove and contracted for a new one in Bayville. We would be able to moor our boat in Mill Neck Creek which was still very clean. The elementary school would be only a couple of blocks away and the beach was near enough for us to walk to; a very important consideration since I still did not drive and the children were reaching an age when they wanted to swim every day. The move was made at the end of July and we spent the rest of the summer exploring nearby: Northport, Huntington and Oyster Bays and Cold Spring Harbor. Beautiful still, in those days, all of them have deteriorated with the great increase in population on Long Island.

Realizing that Marie would need a bunk for the next season and that there was not a spare foot of space in the boat we sadly made the decision to sell HOLIDAY. She had served us well and since she was in such good condition it did not take long to find a buyer. The Steelcraft had been a good first boat with well-thought out use of space for her size, but the ride was pretty rough and the condensation which formed every night from all our breathing humanity drove us forever from the ranks of steel or fiber-glass boat owners. We decided that our next boat would be made of wood!

2

ELCO CRUISETTE
1928 34′

"DOROTHY"
Power: Chrysler Crown 125 h.p. gas

1957

Winter 1956/57 found us settling into a new home in a new community and looking for another boat. Joe and I had always made our rounds of the boat yards "en famille," but now we had two children in school: Michele in second grade where she was already leading her class, and Joey very reluctantly in Kindergarten, as well as two toddlers, Renee and Jeff, and baby Marie at home. I had to be home on school days, so Joe often went alone to follow up boat ads and tour the boatyards. Looking for boats in the winter was discouraging ... canvas covers were tightly tied and boatyards often locked, their sensible owners gone south, but as spring approached Joe got to know every emerging craft on Long Island.

Early in April he was driving along Woodcleft Canal in Freeport when he spotted the *For Sale* sign on DOROTHY, a well preserved 34′ 1928 Elco Cruisette. He had seen the boat earlier while her owner was getting her ready to launch, but at that time she was not yet on the market. Her owner was retired and living nearby, so it didn't take long for Joe to get a complete tour of the boat as well as a long story about her restoration.

He burst into the house just about beside himself with excitement.

"Get your checkbook, honey, I've found IT!"

Terrified lest someone else put a deposit on the boat before we could get there, he rushed us to Freeport as soon as the children got home from school. Scarcely pausing for breath he recounted the beauties, charms, layout, history and possibilities of his find. Today, when I look at pictures of the Elco, especially in black and white, she looks like an old-fashioned houseboat ... how we do get spoiled ... but then she really looked beautiful to me, too.

During World War II, almost every boat that could float had been commandeered by the Coast Guard and put into service patrolling the coast. That had been the final indignity for many irreplaceable wooden boats; the depression had already deprived many of them of the tender, loving care so vital to their longevity. At war's end they were unrestorable; many ended neglected and rotting in countless yards all along the coast.

I do not know how, but for some reason DOROTHY had escaped this fate; she was hidden securely in an ancient shed by the shore, her bottom drawing life giving moisture from the earthen floor, where her owner spent the war years painstakingly rebuilding and restoring his treasure. When I first saw DOROTHY her varnished mahogany was almost completely sound inside and out. The upper and lower berths, port and starboard, were covered in red leather (not plastic). The leaded glass in her varnished china closet sparkled. She did not leak one drop; her cedar hull was smooth and tight. In a word, she was a wooden boat lover's dream come true!

While she had only four berths, the same as the Steelcraft, her wheelhouse had a folding table and her aft cockpit was completely enclosed by canvas curtains. Foam pads and sleeping bags could be spread in these two areas at night to provide plenty of needed sleeping space: Joey would have the wheelhouse, Joe and I the back deck under canvas. We had $2,000 left from the sale of the Steelcraft. We would have to borrow $1,500 to buy the Elco. Looking back, I can hardly believe how possible dreams were in the days before inflation.

Since the boat was already painted, varnished, and in the water, spring commissioning consisted of vacuuming and polishing and the installation of our housekeeping and personal gear. We took a few trial runs in the Freeport area to make sure the engine was running well, and waited for a weekend with a favorable weather forecast. Bringing the boat "home" to our mooring in Mill Neck Creek would involve cruising into waters clearly marked "Atlantic Ocean" for the first time, and since we went nowhere without our children we wanted to be very cautious.

Our friend, George, was working at the power plant in Island Park and living on his boat at a dock there, so he planned to make the trip part way around with us. We met at Woodcleft Canal on a Friday afternoon and ran down Long Creek, then, heading east at Point Lookout, we ran the Sloop Channel past Jones Beach, Tobay Beach (where we had often gone to swim in the ocean) and Captree Island, finally anchoring off Fire Island near Saltaire.

It was dark when we arrived and we almost ran aground several times before finding safe anchorage. Fire Island was in the opposite direction for our trip home, but we felt that since we had never been there we didn't want to miss the opportunity. We also thought it would be more enjoyable to anchor for the night among these barrier islands rather than in industrial areas to the west.

The weather cooperated; Saturday dawned clear and calm. We retraced our course of the previous evening, enjoying the salt marshes and jubilant sea birds in the early morning light. Since the channel is narrow with frequent shoals we concentrated on staying well within the channel markers. Groundings are all too common. We threw a line to one unfortunate sailboat skipper who was rocking his small boat in an effort to free her from a bank.

Our course took us through Reynold's Channel to East Rockaway Inlet and into the ocean which was calm as a millpond, along Rockaway Beach, past Coney Island where I had often walked on visits to an elementary school chum, Joanne Cahn Gillen, after she moved to Brooklyn, and into the Narrows. George waved his farewell at that point and returned to his dock while we continued through now familiar waters enjoying the Statue of Liberty and Manhattan's towers again.

As we pulled into the East River a big tugboat sped by us and we discovered what folks mean when they refer to the "Elco Roll." There were two deck chairs stowed overhead between the frames of the roof which extended over the cockpit. When the boat started to roll, down crashed the chairs! The former owner must have used the boat only in completely protected waters or he would never have stowed his chairs so dangerously. Everyone was inside at the time so no one was hurt; needless to say, the chairs stayed down. We learned to keep a sharp lookout for speeding boats to avoid being caught in their wakes.

Our worst mishap as a result of the boat's tendency to roll occurred while we were anchored in a harbor. I had just put eight loaded dinner plates on the table when a big, twin-screw Chris Craft roared by within feet of our bow. The dinner crashed to the floor and we were all knocked off our feet; I swear that the boat rocked for twenty minutes! Joe was so mad that he got into the dinghy and pursued that outlaw to his mooring and roundly cussed him out. The contrite skipper begged Joe not to report him, promising to mend his ways; he already had received two summons for similar incidents, and Joe relented. I wish that scoundrel had thought to pay for our lost dinner.

With their round bottoms all Elcos roll easily, but ours seemed especially tender. During her lifetime the heavy Gray engine had been replaced by a much lighter Chrysler Crown, her open wheelhouse had been enclosed with a heavy mahogany and glass structure and a flying bridge added on top. As we discovered, design changes made by owners without good advice can make a boat not only uncomfortable but unsafe. Throughout our ownership every cruise involved the most careful stowage of every possession and the most earnest avoidance of any rough water in the attempt to keep the children safe from spills.

For our vacation cruise in '57 we took the Hudson River to the Federal Lock at Troy, but instead of heading north to Champlain as we had previously, we turned west at Waterford. Our destination: Lake Oneida, via the Erie Canal and Mohawk River. As usual, our friend, George, made the trip with us taking his own boat and a couple of friends.

The first five locks on the canal are called the "Waterford Flight" with good reason: in less than two miles our boats were raised 165 feet. It's very exciting to ride into those deep locks, watch the huge doors close behind you, and hanging onto the ladders on the rough, dungeon-like walls, feel the boat slowly lifted to the next level.

Beyond Lock 6 the canal becomes the Mohawk River and there are several places where the remains of the original, abandoned canal can be seen ... it looks so tiny. Walking the banks we thought of the countless immigrants who, often sick and always overworked, had dug them by hand· so many years before. Walter D. Edmonds wrote three wonderful novels about the Erie Canal and the Mohawk River: DRUMS ALONG THE MOHAWK, ROME HAUL and ERIE WATER. Reading them made the whole area come alive for me!

One day while I was having a turn at the wheel I strayed from the center of the channel. Quite suddenly I realized that the boat was not moving; I put her in neutral and called to Joe. He took the wheel and had to agree ... we could go nowhere! There did not seem to be any mechanical problem so Joe took to the dinghy to check out the bottom.

Poking under the boat with an oar Joe felt a solid concrete wall which he surmised was an old lock or bridge support. Our bow was resting lightly on this immovable object. There are no tides to free unwary navigators on the canal and I was feeling very guilty about our plight but Joe was undaunted. He hadn't worked for Al Marra for all those years for nothing! After studying the drift of the current he had me throw him a long rope which I had fastened to the bow cleat. He tied the rope to the dinghy seat and rowed at an angle to the wall which would put the current to use. Rowing mightily but hardly moving he gradually twisted the boat till it fell off the cement wall. We all cheered as he towed us to safety in the center of the channel.

Our destination, Sylvan Beach on Lake Oneida, was 130 miles from Waterford but it seemed farther. The weather was too hot for comfort, there were swarms of flies and mosquitoes, safe anchorages and stores were hard to find, and we didn't trust the canal water for swimming. Recent cruising guides provide good information on presently available services, but we just had our charts and intuition.

The ELCO on the Erie Canal. Joe on the bridge with Joey.
Bumpers ready for locking through.

It was a relief to reach Sylvan Beach with its amusement park, clean swimming and full services. All the kids, big and little, enjoyed the bumper cars and roller coaster. Our plans had called for crossing the lake, but we waited three days during which the wind never ceased. The lake was foaming with white caps. We decided it was wiser to skip the crossing rather than chance being stuck on the far side, so we started the return trip with time to spare.

Lots of summer was still before us when we got home, so we made several trips to Connecticut ports. We especially enjoyed Essex with its beautiful old homes and interesting shops. In one little store the children discovered Swedish Ivy, sold in child size pots. We still have some of the descendants of that ivy. We made our first trip to Mystic Seaport where we learned much about the early days of shipbuilding. Our love for New England grew.

When we hauled the boat in October, we looked forward to a busy winter. Joe gave the boat his usual thorough going over from stem to stern. I was busier than ever with three little school children and two toddlers. Helping with the local PTA started about this time and I had to get our home rearranged to make room for still another addition to our family; this would make the six I'd always vowed I'd have. During that pregnancy I made the hooked rug which now lies in front of our wood stove.

1958

Son Jimmy (who just graduated from Stonybrook University on Long Island as an Electrical Engineer ... and bicycle racer extraordinaire) was born on February 16 ... a healthy, happy boy who evened up the family at three boys and three girls!

Old hands at taking babies to sea, we still planned to cruise to Lake Champlain once again in '58. Even though he painted and varnished the whole boat himself, Joe was ready to launch by Memorial Day as always. The boat looked really beautiful; Joe had changed her name to JEANNE, and I felt honored and proud ... of Joe and of the boat.

The children were reaching an age when they eagerly anticipated our long annual cruise. During the work-a-day year Joe worked long hours, often getting home after the kids were in bed. During vacations he tried to make up for it: hiking, swimming, shopping, playing hilarious bridge and rowing them around harbors and creeks by the hour, sharing ideas and experiences.

As soon as school ended we were ready to leave for Lake Champlain.

When we cast off from our mooring everything seemed to be working well. Spirits were soaring. As we passed Oak Neck Point on our way to Glen Cove to rendezvous with George, we ran into a sudden bank of fog which cut our visibility to nearly zero. Joe reduced throttle and I took the wheel trying to hold to the compass course for the bell off Matinecock Pt. while he hushed the children and tried to see and hear through the fog. Suddenly a strange noise from under the aft deck joined the quiet thump of the engine, throttled down for creeping in fog. Joe lifted the hatch to reveal a broken rudder cable.

His many years of experience fixing cars and trucks and making do in emergencies came to his aid as did his good supply of tools. In minutes he had clamped a patch on the rudder cable. The fog lifted as quickly as it had descended and we found ourselves right on course. Pretty good for a rudderless boat! We resumed our speed, thankful for the calm sea which had helped us avoid landing on the rockstrewn shore. Superstitution has it that trouble comes in threes ... minutes later, the third!

We had just begun to relax when a strange new noise interrupted the steady beat of the engine and the soft rush of the water. This time it came from the engine. Joe lifted the engine box and listened in stunned disbelief to the rapping sound of the bearing insert on No. 3 piston. Six pairs of wide eyes, six anxiously beating hearts awaited the verdict from the chief engineer. Jimmy was too little to care.

Beginning at upper left and clockwise:
Michele, Joey, Renee, Marie, Jimmy and Jeff.
The first six ... a happy crew ... in 1958.

"Sorry, kids ... this old engine will never make it to Lake Champlain." We all held back our tears, but we were mighty quiet. There we were, all ready for a wonderful vacation. Something none of us ever expected: a broken down engine!

Joe disconnected the spark plug wire to No. 3. He said we could still run but we would have to go slow and stay in completely protected waters, since we couldn't know how long the engine would last.

Slowly we limped into Glen Cove where we met George and told him he would have to make the trip without us. I can still remember how heart-broken the children looked as we waved farewell to the lucky travelers.

Joe and I held a consultation and decided that we would not abort the vacation by hauling the boat for repairs. Since the engine was salt-water cooled and quite old we decided that it should be replaced; but that was a job for the winter, not for vacation time.

Instead of merely returning to our home port, we haltingly motored the few miles farther into Huntington Bay and dropped anchor behind a beautiful sand spit in Lloyd Harbor. We spent our two weeks right there, walking the beach, swimming, rowing, reading and playing bridge by candlelight. We had our bird book, a guide to wildflowers and a shell book: we studied all the natural world. Every third day or so, depending on the weather, we started up the engine and idled into Huntington Harbor for food and ice. After a few such trips at slow speeds the battery refused to start the boat, but we were saved by the fact that the previous owner had installed a hand crank on the engine. Accustomed as he was to starting cement mixers with a crank, Joe was able to muster the considerable strength required to turn the engine.

In some ways it turned out to be one of our most relaxing vacations. After we got over our disappointment at missing the trip, we discovered the pure pleasure of just living aboard.

When Joe's vacation was almost over we picked a beautiful, still day and idled the boat back to Mill Neck Creek. No more cruising for that year. We went home, cut the grass, picked up the branches in our acre of woods, did the laundry and tended the vegetable garden ... Joe went back to work. When the next weekend arrived we moved onto the boat. It was fun just living in the creek, clean water all around. Sunday evening I convinced Joe that the children and I should stay on the boat during the week. We still had only one car and we lived over a mile from the shore; it was a long walk for the children when we wanted to go to the beach (every sunny day).

Mornings I packed Joe's lunch as usual and rowed him quickly ashore. After breakfast I rowed ashore with all the children and we spent a couple of hours walking the beach and swimming. After lunch aboard or a picnic ashore the little ones had a nap while the older children rowed around the boat in the dinghy or put fishing lines out from the mother ship. Naps over and dinner preparations made we'd all go ashore for more swimming and play with young friends at the community beach. Since we all lived in bathing suits and there's little housework on a boat, I had one of the easiest summers of my adult life, in spite of having six children to care for. (Michele, the oldest, would be nine that November). We went home a couple of times a week to take care of the yard, shop for food, do laundry and give everyone a good bath and shampoo.

We hauled the boat in September that year in order to have time to change the engine before covering the boat for the winter. Joe located a rebuilt Chrysler Crown and began unbuttoning the old engine; then he built an A frame from which to suspend a chain hoist.

When all was in readiness he asked a neighbor, Walter Waas, to help him lift the engine out. They went off in Walter's car one evening about 8:00 o'clock. Joe said they would be home about 10, but 11 o'clock came and then 12. Joe is the kind of husband who always calls me when he's delayed, so when I didn't hear from him I started to get worried. By midnight I was concerned enough to break a lifelong rule. I left our children sleeping alone and drove the few miles to the boatyard, thankful that Joe had left the car. I knew something was wrong.

When I climbed the ladder into the boat you never saw two men so happy to see a woman. When the engine had been hoisted nearly to the top, the A frame had slipped. Joe and Walter had grabbed it quickly enough to keep the engine from crashing through the hull, but they were both immobilized, unable to move. They had been holding on like that for over an hour ... praying someone would come down to the boatyard, thinking of and discarding one idea after another, wondering how long they could hold on.

At Joe's direction I went looking for heavy planks to place under the engine, then I lowered it while they braced the A frame. I hurried home to the children to find them all sleeping peacefully, while Joe and Walter stayed behind to jockey the engine out onto the deck where the boatyard crane could reach it in the morning. I still feel a little guilty when I remember leaving the children alone that night. If anything had happened to them no boat in the world could have consoled me. I should have called the police and had them check the boatyard ... it was probably on their patrol schedule. I was too shy ... my mistake.

Long before winter Joe had the new engine neatly installed and the winter cover secured. By the time Christmas came I realized that there would be another addition to the family. Since the baby was due in August we decided that it would be sensible to cruise only on Long Island in '59. The new baby would sleep in a bassinet in '59 and by 1960 Jimmy could be moved into the wheelhouse with Joey and Jeff. The boat would still be big enough! At least, we thought so.

1959

As summer progressed I began to realize that this was not my usual kind of pregnancy. I got bigger and bigger, more and more uncomfortable. We went cruising every weekend but stayed in ports fairly close to home. I outgrew my maternity clothes. I finally had to use an elastic band to hold up my pants ... threading it through the button holes and around the buttons. One day while standing on the bow in all my glory I reached out to throw a line over a dock bollard and ... you guessed it ... my elastic broke! It is just not easy to dock while losing your pants. I was lucky though, the dock was deserted and Joe rushed down from the bridge to help me. We both had a good laugh.

Another day was no laughing matter. We were anchored in the sand hole on Lloyd's Neck when I had an unforgettable scare. Joe and all the children were beachcombing and since they were having fun Joe was in no hurry to get back. He knew I needed the rest. Well, I was resting, at first, but I got up to get a drink and fell to the floor absolutely paralyzed and in awful pain. I tried to drag myself to the bell or lift myself high enough to signal for help, but it was no use. I couldn't move at all. Trembling with fear and frustration, lying immobilized on the back deck, I thought I'd die ... or lose my baby. I was almost hysterical by the time I heard the sound of oars and the children's chatter. Joe hurried the children below, telling Michele to take charge, and tried to help me move. Gradually the spasm ended. I imagine that the baby had pressed on some critical nerve, because the paralysis did not recur. After that, Joe and the children stayed in sight of the boat and I waved to them regularly so they would know I was all right.

I went to the hospital on August 14th, and we found out why my pregnancy had been so difficult ... we had twins! The beautiful, blonde twins I had always hoped for. Elaine, named after Joe's mother weighed 5½ lbs., and my namesake, little Jeanne weighed 4½ lbs. At this point we had eight children under 10 years of age.

Elaine had to remain in the hospital for a complete exchange transfusion and Jeanne stayed to put on weight and to give her lungs time to mature. I went home without a baby! How miserable. I brought Elaine home a few days later but it was almost a month before Jeanne was released. Regaining my strength and coping with tiny twins pushed boating to the background for me that fall, but Joe kept pondering the alternatives: sell the boat, or make more room ... somehow!

Over and over again we came back to the same thought. Wasn't it too bad that the whole bow of the Elco was taken up by tanks ... gas on top, water below. Beautiful copper tanks, made to fit, with gasketed inspection plates facing an access door. Without the gas tank a good, child-sized bunk could be built in the bow ... but, where would we carry the gas?

1960

About the middle of March Joe untied the canvas at the stern of the boat and climbed aboard with a tape measure; a way would be found. The stern of the Elco had two built-in fish wells which we never used for fish. Joe decided to take them out. Once the whole space was gutted he measured it carefully and drew a sketch for a gas tank which would take advantage of every inch, then he went to a metal shop to have it built.

He drained the gas in the bow tank and then filled the tank with water, flushing it out several times. With the boat well ventilated he removed the inspection plate on the tank, then, slowly but surely, cut, folded, bent and compressed the tank until it could be taken out through the door.

He cut plywood to fit on top of the water tank, drilled holes in the door to provide ventilation and installed a light overhead. I cut foam rubber to fit, covered it and made a bumper to go all around. It's true, we had to go through the head to get to the little nursery, but it was a safe, cozy baby space.

That winter I got my first washer-dryer. No more laundromat for me twice a week. People who own boats often do without lots of other things (like clothes and new cars). We also finished a basement room for the two oldest boys ... our three bedroom ranch house was stretched to capacity. With great foresight we had bought an 8' picnic table for our dining area and with two high chairs we dined in style!

When we started cruising in the spring of 1960 both twins were still small enough for a bassinet, but there was not room for two. What to do? I brought two big tissue cartons home from the supermarket, cut them down and made cushions. "Voila!" Two portable beds which could be moved easily while providing safe, draftfree sleeping. Only one twin could sleep in the bow-bed at a time, since they played and kept each other awake. Since we always kept the whole boat spotlessly clean, the boat was one big playpen for their waking hours, and with six adoring, big brothers and sisters there was always someone willing and able to guard the companion-way.

Elaine, Grandmother St. Andre, Jeanne and a proud Dad!

Our two years of cruising alone had broken our habit of traveling with another boat. From now on we would go on our own way. As we planned for that summer we decided we wanted to explore the eastern end of Long Island Sound and Shelter Island. Our harbor and the other local anchorages were getting crowded and we'd had enough of Lake Champlain. Time for a change.

During our August vacation we went east, ducked into Mattituck Inlet on the north shore of Long Island and spent a couple of days walking in all directions from that safe vantage point. We went on around Orient Point, through Plum Gut to Dering Harbor for shopping and refueling at Picozzi's, then around Shelter Island into Coecles Harbor where we could swim and walk quiet beaches. Up to that point the weather had been ideal: sunny and calm, perfect cruising even for an old Elco.

Suddenly the wind switched. Day after day it blew with fury from the northeast. We were trapped in that then isolated harbor. We didn't know if there was a store and Joe was afraid to leave us long enough to look for one, or even to leave the boat. After some days, with food and time running low we talked ourselves into making a break for Dering Harbor.

Joe was on the flying bridge as usual with our two oldest sons ... our first mistake ... too much weight too high. As soon as we cleared the entrance we knew we were in trouble. This entrance channel is quite narrow with extensive shoals on both sides for a considerable distance. The shoals combined with the stiff wind created steep seas which tossed us unmercifully. It was too rough for Joe and the boys to climb down from the bridge, yet their weight up there was making our rolling perilous. The other six children and I were all life-jacketed, huddled together on the back deck, singing at the tops of our voices ... "Michael, Row the Boat Ashore," and "Glory, Glory, Hallelujah!" We were ready to be cast into the sea. There was no way we could turn back ... we hung on, praying and singing; Joe strained every nerve watching each wave, trying to direct the boat so that it would survive the onslaught.

Finally we reached deeper water, but the seas were still too steep to allow us to proceed around the island. Bow buried under every wave, white water swirling over the trunk cabin, our only possible heading was toward Orient Point. As we neared Long Beach we finally got into the lee of the land and were able to hug the coast back past Long Beach Point and into Dering Harbor. The danger was past, but we had learned a lesson. Right then we resolved that since we were going to cruise the coast with our children we would need a real sea-going boat.

A time of decisions once again. After seeing the lovely, uncrowded farmlands, beaches and harbors of eastern Long Island, we decided to sell our Bayville house and move east; and after our brush with disaster in the Elco we would sell it and buy or build a boat really designed for offshore cruising.

The Elco with its full displacement hull and narrow beam had been an economical boat to operate since it used only about three gallons of gas an hour to move at about nine knots. It was small enough to get into low-overhead boatyards where Joe could do all the work on her, both indispensable considerations with our income and responsibilities. Cruising rivers, bays and harbors she had served us well, but with her straight sides and lack of flare forward, not to mention her age, she was not safe in the ocean.

That fall we wet-stored JEANNE in the Glen Cove Marina and put her on the market. She was beautiful still, but we wanted to go to sea. Like the frog who left his safe puddle for the big pond, we were often to find ourselves in over our depth in the years to come.

Fifteen years later while walking in a boatyard near Threemile Harbor we came upon our old treasure, engine missing, cotton hanging from sprung planks: a sorry derelict. We often wonder how she reached that lonely, forsaken end. While she was having her troubles, we were having hard years, too.

September 1959 on the Elco
Jeanne brings the new twins aboard for the first time.
Standing, l to r: Jeff, Joey, Renee, Marie, Jim and Michele

3

CLAYTON FLETCHER
DOWNEAST CRUISER
1962 42'

"JEANNE"
Power: Lehman Ford 120 h.p. 6 cylinder diesel

1961

Once Joe and I got an idea into our heads there was no stopping us. We were determined to move east so we could cruise in the clean waters surrounding Suffolk County, as well as to own a boat that could safely take our big family cruising into New England's coastal waters. Both dreams took some doing!

We put our Bayville house up for sale just at the time when the real estate market was feeling the backlash from President Kennedy's steel problems; it took almost a year to sell it. Dozens of car trips out to Suffolk were required before we found a property we liked and could afford: a small house that needed lots of work but had almost an acre of land with a 185' bulkhead on a beautiful, dredged canal. We moved in just before Christmas.

That winter sorely tested our courage: the pipes froze, the canal froze, a window blew in during a snow storm, our feet froze on the uninsulated floors; our tiny house was crowded (cozy) and leaning toward the canal, but it was a waterfront home ... there was no place to go but UP!

Now to find a real offshore boat that would sleep ten. George had also sold his Steelcraft and gone to Nova Scotia where he had George Boudreau build him a 39′ fishing boat for less than $4,000. While his new boat was quite rough, it was a safe "sea boat" with its good flare forward and its large, stable working deck aft. The fishermen of Canada are not interested in fancy boats, but they do go into the ocean all year long in all kinds of weather. We decided to look for a boat builder in Nova Scotia, too; before we could implement that plan we saw an ad in the MAINE COAST FISHERMAN: Clayton Fletcher on Campobello Island would build for work or pleasure. We wrote to him for prices. When Joe went up to see Clayton he had just finished building a 36′ lobster boat; it looked very good to Joe, and the price was in the ballpark.

1962

By March, 1962 Joe and Clayton had agreed on a design for a 42′ boat that would sleep EVERYONE: upper and lower berths, port and starboard in the bow, two couches with pipe berths above in the main cabin and an extension couch-berth in the wheelhouse. The head compartment would be in the main cabin opposite a large hanging locker, and the galley would be along the starboard side of the wheelhouse. After years of cooking below decks in the Steelcraft and Elco I would enjoy having my galley at the center of activity. We also planned to have a canvas cover for the large cockpit so the kids could spread out on cold or rainy days.

The only boat-building ingredients native to Campobello Island were reasonably priced labor and some wood; everything else had to be brought over from the states. Every pay day, instead of getting a baby-sitter and going to dinner or the movies, we'd go to the Baldwin Boat Basin where Joe would pick out some piece of hardware or other equipment for the new boat. When he could stand the suspense no longer he'd load all his treasures into the car and head for Wilson's Beach. Joey and Jeff were his usual companions on those weekends.

The International Bridge to Campobello Island was built the year after our boat; in 1962 the island was reached by means of a two-part "ferry" consisting of a big, old, wooden barge secured to a lobster boat. It carried six or eight cars. The skipper of this contraption had to take a course far up or down stream from the landing site depending on which way the tide was running and then open the throttle wide to compensate for the swift tidal current. There was no landing ramp on the island side, the cars just rode up the stony beach. It felt like the end of the world.

Joe and the boys made many exciting trips across during that year while they watched Clayton build our boat. Each time Joe came back more in love with Maine.

There was no motel at Wilson's Beach and Clayton was a bachelor living with his family, so Joe and the boys would bed down at the home of Clayton's right hand man, Dell. His tiny house was perched high on a hill with a view far out to sea; dried cod and pollock were hung in the little entry porch; the bright, sunny kitchen was warmed by a huge wood cook stove. The parlor stove which heated the rest of the house was seldom lit so the bedrooms were icy but the beds were piled high with handmade quilts. Joe will never forget the early sunrises in that welcoming house.

On one spring trip Joe arrived in the midst of a celebration. The weather had finally cleared enough to allow the men to fish their traps and they had returned with hundreds of pounds of lobster ... the joyful partying lasted all weekend. Joe brought home two huge lobsters (Canada had no size limit, I guess) which he turned loose on the cellar floor; their still lively antics enthralled the children. They had never seen such creatures. I was sorry that I had to be their executioner.

In July Joe bought a used Chris Craft engine for $500, rented a U-Haul trailer and brought the engine up to Clayton. Our plan for the boat had called for a raised deck forward; we thought the hull would be deep enough to eliminate the need for a trunk cabin. We had hoped to reduce construction costs while avoiding one very common source of leaks in wood boats. When Joe saw the outcome of this plan the wheelhouse had already been built, but the head room forward was not adequate. The wheelhouse had to be removed and a trunk cabin built. Before we were finished we had $7,000 invested in the boat ... not much by today's standards, but a lot to us in 1962! We learned the hard way how amateur architects can fail; even with a professional you are taking a chance that the design will turn out the way you picture it.

By the time the changes were made it was October. Clayton wrote that the boat was ready and then could find no one willing to deliver it; we did not then consider ourselves knowledgeable enough to bring the boat home, especially in October. We asked Clayton to buy a canvas and cover the boat; delivery would have to wait till spring.

Before the boat was covered I managed to get one trip to the island. We divided the children between the two grandmothers and Joe and I had a second honeymoon. After hearing so much about Dell and his wife I really enjoyed meeting them at last and being able to thank them for all the hospitality they had shown my family. Dell's wife let me help her work on a new quilt, and so I brought home a valuable skill. To this day I never buy a blanket, I make a quilt! Their house was just as Joe had described it ... the sky and sea as blue ... their food as tasty and satisfying ... the kitchen as warm.

1963

In April, Clayton found an island fisherman who was willing to deliver the JEANNE. She came through customs on April 16. Her arrival was anticipated with almost the fervor usually reserved for a new baby ... the reality of that arrival was something else. The long, hard winter had taken its toll of the paint job. During the trip down an engine oil fitting had leaked and the bilges were full of oil. Even worse, the engine had over-heated! None of the trim had been bedded down and all the moldings were holding water. Instead of a spanking new boat, we had what looked like a lot of work! We surveyed our house, our boat and our finances; this time we really were in over our heads!

That year we worked harder than ever. Joe jacked up our sloping house, chinked and grouted the foundation and insulated the floors. He installed a bilge pump with an automatic float in the cellar; the house was just twenty feet from the bulkhead and every high tide came up! I painted, wallpapered, made curtains and raised vegetables along with children. The boat was tied up in front of the house and every day that the weather permitted we caulked, bedded, sanded and painted. We took a few short runs, but it was hard to take time out to play when there was so much work; the engine gave ample warning that the over-heating had caused serious damage. We borrowed again, this time to replace the gas engine with a six cylinder Ford Diesel which Joe installed himself.

1964

After a year of endless effort the boat was really beautiful ... completely repainted inside and out. I had made and covered cushions for all the bunks and made sleeping bags for all the children. The dreamed of cruises could begin at last.

The freshly painted wheelhouse on JEANNE. My braided rugs.

Since our home was on a canal off Flanders Bay, our weekend cruising encompassed Great and Little Peconic Bays while for longer trips Shelter Island and Fishers Island both offered many fine, clean harbors in which to drop anchor. Our first weekend cruise was to West Neck Harbor on Shelter Island. The lure there was Shell Beach, which we hoped would match its name; anyone with young children knows how a beach full of shells holds their interest. The girls especially liked Jingle shells which they strung into countless necklaces and wind chimes.

The weekend got off to an exciting start ... when entering this harbor the deep water is found by hugging the beach to port ... but who could imagine that you had to stay THAT close! We grounded.

Joe told the whole family to go up and stand as close to the bow as possible. I thought that was pretty silly but he insisted, so all nine of us marched forward while he reversed the engine and applied full throttle. Daddy was right again; off the shoal slid the bow-heavy JEANNE. We very cautiously explored the creek into West Neck enjoying the beautiful homes along the way.

We spent many happy weekends anchored in West Harbor on Fishers Island. We loved the peaceful island life and walked for hours on its quiet roads and shores. Sometimes the yacht club would have a mooring available which made our long hikes more worry-free; it's hard to really trust an anchor.

There were so many new towns to explore, new boats to admire, new courses to run; we were soon to discover, however, that in many ways it had been easier to cruise when the children were small. Then, they thought boat trips were the greatest adventure and were content to spend weekends and vacations with the family ... swimming, hiking and playing bridge.

Beginning in '63, each year would find another child entering the dark tunnel that is adolescence. They began to have baby-sitting jobs, lawns to cut, friends from whom they were more and more inseparable. Little by little we altered our cruising plans to fit in with their commitments. While we owned this boat we only cruised as far as Watch Hill, exploring the Pawcatuck River to Westerly for the first time, as well as making further, very enjoyable visits to the Connecticut and Mystic Rivers and Stonington, Connecticut.

The twins were due to start school in September and the general consensus was: "eight is enough," but an all-wise providence had other plans. I was pregnant again.

That winter we stored the boat right in the water at our own dock where we could keep on working to make it better as time allowed. One winter day while Joe was working on the boat he slipped and plunged into the icy water. Though he hit his head quite sharply he was not knocked out and he climbed up without help. I will never forget the sight of him as he came through the kitchen door ... dripping wet and covered with blood. He had caught his ear in the fall and the lobe was cut halfway through. I helped him change and drove him to the emergency room where a talented surgeon sewed him up. Only a small scar remains to recall what could have been a tragic accident.

On another day I was spraying cuprinol into joints so Joe could re-bed the moldings. I got too close to my work and some of the cuprinol splashed into my eyes. I never should have been working without goggles. I was lucky that I had clean water handy ... I threw water into my eyes and quickly flushed them out, then groped my way ashore and into the house. I called my neighbor, Jeanne Pflum, and she took me to the emergency room. No permanent damage resulted, but how stupid and careless!

In September '64 the twins went off to Kindergarten ... I was alone at home in the mornings. The first time if fifteen years ... how restful ... and lonely.

1965

In February we were blessed with one more son, Paul, and found as have so many other parents that this last child had a special place to fill in our lives. Once we had nine children we realized that there was no way we could fit even one more bed in our tiny house; an addition was imperative. That was an alternative not available with the boat. That summer we hired Roy Stakey to build a big addition which doubled our space. He also replaced all the old windows with Andersons, re-roofed, and sided old and new with easy-care cypress board and batten.

SKATING on the ice in front of our re-modeled house and re-finished boat.
Back: Jeff, Jeanne, Joe, Joey
Front: Jeanie, Marie and Elaine

More and more we found that we had to be content with day cruises; the teens were too busy with their lives and still too young to leave alone. Once Joey got his driver's license we found a way to enjoy the boat with all the family. Joe and I would take the younger children aboard and head out to Greenport or Sag Harbor on Saturday mornings; the teenagers would work at their assorted jobs, and Joey would drive them out to join us for dinner and possibly a movie. They'd spend the night and whoever was free would go back on the boat with us Sunday evening.

Looking back I think those years would have been easier if we had not even tried to accommodate our big family for overnight cruising. It would have been less expensive for us and more enjoyable for the children if we had owned a fleet of assorted day boats: sail boat, canoe, speed boat and fishing dory could easily have tied to our 185' dock and given all the children opportunities to experience the other pleasures of the water. Joe and I tended to be protective, however, so we would have had even more gray hairs if they had all been out in different boats scattered over the bay.

Once Joey saved some money from his landscaping business he bought a Thompson runabout for water skiing. As soon as he was able Jimmy bought a bigger and faster Stamas and learned to be an accomplished skier.

1966

When Paul was about a year old I realized that I had a lump in my breast which did not go away. I soon forced myself to have a biopsy done ... the lump was cancerous. I had to have a mastectomy. Since my father had died from cancer when I was only thirteen I had always feared that killer disease. Boats did not seem important. I just wanted to live. In the depression following that surgery I tried to re-order my life's priorities.

I had always hoped to start a day care center some day; all of my experience with children seemed too valuable to waste. At that point I thought: "Now or Never!" By September PINE TREE NURSERY SCHOOL (later PINE TREE DAY NURSERY, INC.) was a reality. My life was full once again. The day care center solved many problems for us: it took my mind off my health (which has since been excellent), it enabled me to lift some of the burden of our support from my husband's shoulders, we could employ any of our children who needed jobs thus enabling them to save for college, and I could take my own baby, Paul, then eighteen months old, to work with me. In the years since, the nursery has also solved the problem of loving child care for over two thousand families: an achievement we view with pride and satisfaction. The day care experience is also the subject of another book which I hope to finish soon.

In the meantime Joe kept improving the boat; he took off the mast, added a flying bridge and an opening hatch in the forward bunk room, and covered the planked, cockpit deck with marine plywood. Each year the boat looked better and better, but keeping it that way took lots of time. We found that the exterior plywoods we had used in building were not adequate for marine use, in spite of every care they checked. While we had brought

Clayton everdur bronze screws to fasten the cedar planks of the hull, he had run out of these and finished above the water line with galvanized screws which bled rust through before any season was half over.

While we had hoped that a builder of fishing boats would build a sea-worthy boat we found that design was crucial; we were not completely satisfied with the sea-keeping qualities of this boat. Her bow was too full, her sheer too high and her fore-foot not quite deep enough. We found docking and even mooring difficult since she had a tendency to blow off if there was any wind. That's not much of a problem for fishermen, they don't worry about scratches, but we never wanted to mar our perfect paint job. In the steep chop on Long Island Sound she pounded in a way that was uncomfortable though not unsafe, while in the longer waves offshore she rode easier. We started to get restless. Perhaps some other kind of boat would suit us more.

1970

More and more dissatisfied, Joe decided. We would sell the JEANNE and look for one of the really fine old classic yachts, perhaps one with an aft cabin so we could have some privacy. Those exquisite older boats always had fine woods and beautiful workmanship ... once restored such a boat would be a treasure.

While we owned this boat our four oldest children had grown from little kids to young adults. Michele was off to college at Mount Holyoke (class of '71), Joey was at Harpur College and Renee was just finishing high school.

We had been tempered by adversity: raising children during a youth revolution, fighting for health and solvency. Realization dawned ... health is the only real wealth ... any boat is just the icing on the cake.

*Elaine, Paul, Joe
and Jeanie on the
stern of JEANNE.*

4

NEVINS COMMUTER YACHT
1930 54'

"PRETTY BETTY"
(renamed LADY JEANNE)
Power: General Motors 471 160 h.p. twin diesels

It is almost a standing joke with boat owners that as soon as they get a boat paid for it's time to look for a new one; as a breed, we tend to think that the grass is always greener ... and that bigger just has to be better. Even though we didn't need more space, with so many adolescents aboard, we really started to long for more privacy. Wouldn't it be lovely to have an aft stateroom where Joe and I could "get away from it all?" Though the older children were off to college or working we wanted those children who were still cruising to enjoy the trips but they too wanted privacy for their own music and conversation. We refused to listen to the Beatles and they found nothing enjoyable about Frank Sinatra and Perry Como.

We had always been attracted to the beautiful old yachts: Matthews, Nevins, Elcos, Wheelers and Consolidateds; we decided to look for one of them. Having agreed to search for a larger boat we knew that considerable money would be required over and above the $9,000 we had realized from the sale of the Fletcher boat. We intended to buy a good boat: one that would last our lifetimes, see us through child rearing and finish as a comfortable and thrifty early retirement home. Joe was driving an oil truck and my day care center gave me a small salary but no profit, though it provided needed jobs for our teenagers. No source of adequate dollars there. The only way we could raise enough cash was by selling our waterfront home and moving into the apartment above our day nursery. With our family shrinking as rapidly as it had grown we would be able to manage.

It had proven increasingly difficult to supervise the children after school while I worked; by combining home and career under one roof I would be able to do a better job as mother. The waterfront place had been wonderful when the children were small but its acre of oak trees and lawns required many hours of raking and mowing right during the cruising season. No one wanted to do the work. How discouraging after a two-week cruise to face the disaster of a neglected, abandoned, overgrown yard. With scarcely a backward glance the house would be sold. How many times in the years to come we were to wish we could have kept our lovely, private "marina."

Once again the search was on; we hoped to find a big, old yacht that, like our Elco, had been lovingly preserved and restored ... talk about a needle in a haystack! Anyone who has dreamed this dream knows how many cruel disappointments lie in wait, how many long distance calls, auto trips, motel bills and survey fees stand between the dreamer and the dream. People with old boats to sell have to muffle their consciences when dealing with prospective buyers ... we would never go to look at their old treasures if they told us the whole truth. In 1970 we were still naive ... we went the route in innocent, hopeful expectation.

Once we went to Maryland to see an old Elco which her doctor-owner had described as "absolutely beautiful." We took one look at the listing, sorry, older than advertised hag and left without calling the owner. Another time we spent over a hundred dollars to have a 1929 Matthews hauled and surveyed ... the list of structural defects far outweighed the appeal of her lines and accommodations. We couldn't afford to survey every likely prospect; we'd just have to rely on our own judgment. So it went.

During a late summer visit to Yacht Haven West in Connecticut Joe saw writer Sloan Wilson's PRETTY BETTY and came home in love with that 1930, 54' Nevins. At that time Sloan was living aboard with his wife and young daughter; though he had advertised the boat for sale he was still undecided about selling her. He had just re-majored the two G M 471 engines and completely repainted and varnished the whole exterior; the offers he had thus far received would have left him too far in the red.

Soon after that I came across Sloan's book, AWAY FROM IT ALL, which described his search for a livaboard boat and how the Nevins Commuter Yacht (originally owned by Guy Lombardo) had been the rewarding solution for him. He rhapsodized over the beautiful lines of her double planked cedar and honduras mahogany hull, the piano and fireplace in the deckhouse, the bathtub in the forecastle, the spacious aft cabin with its own head and shower. We were entranced.

Though Sloan was hard to pin down we still hoped he would decide to sell; we were determined to keep trying. In the meantime Sloan and his family had gone to Florida with PRETTY BETTY where we wrote to him ... keeping in touch while he decided which way to go with his life ... and we worked at selling our car and finally selling the house.

In an October letter from Florida Sloan was still hedging; he had "five years of my life and almost $50,000 in the boat" ... he would be lucky to sell it for half of his investment, but he needed money for a proposed European junket. At last, he said he would show us the boat if we came south, but not to make a special trip (no guarantees). Joe made plans to drive to Florida, glad of a chance to inspect the boat more fully.

Though it was only April the temperature at Dinner Key was an unbearable 104° when Joe arrived. Sloan gave him a complete tour and history of the boat, took him for an exciting ride into tropical waters and Betty prepared a lovely dinner ... after all of which Joe called me:

"The boat handles beautifully. She cuts through the waves leaving almost no wake. She looks great. The exterior has just been painted but the whole interior needs refinishing. I think Sloan would consider a reasonable offer."

I told him that the most we could offer was $20,000. Sloan countered with $22,500; they drew up a contract. We would just have to cash in our life insurance ... we had nothing else left. The deed was done!

Since Joe could not leave his job and I could not leave my business long enough to bring the boat north, Sloan suggested that a man who had worked on the boat for him might be willing to do it. We contacted this fellow (who shall be nameless) and he agreed to the trip, provided we could wait until his children finished school in June. With his wife and children along the trip would serve as a family vacation and he would only charge us the actual expenses and for any work he performed at $5 per hour ... no delivery fee, as such. Sloan pointed out that the exterior varnish really needed one more coat to protect it from the tropical heat and our delivery man agreed to get that done in the interim and during the trip north as time and weather allowed.

On June 8 we sent him $500 to begin the trip. Anxious weeks followed as we waited to hear from him. On the 28th a call reported trouble with pumps, bad weather delays, more fuel than expected (it was only 25¢ a gallon at that time). We wired an additional $400. By the time the call from Greenport, New York heralded the arrival of our beautiful, old Nevins we were really broke, but excited and happy. Joe and I raced out to accept delivery.

Through all of this I had never seen the Nevins. After reading all about her in Sloan's book and listening to Joe's enthusiasm, I could hardly wait.

When I first caught sight of the boat, her lovely lines struck me at once; I could see why Joe had been captivated, but as we came alongside it was obvious that much was amiss. During the next hour reality overtook us.

The "reliable" delivery man had picked up his in-laws and taken them and his family for a leisurely Bahamas holiday on our boat while we were waiting. He had not found time to do much of the varnishing and he had not cared for it at all.

Anyone who has exterior varnish in a tropical climate must be prepared to hose off the salt and chamois it dry after every run. The bright work that had looked so elegant in April was completely ruined. The boat was down about three inches below the waterline at the bow. The hose on the forward bilge pump had broken; the gate valve was frozen open and since it was located near the water line, more water poured in during every run. All the drawers and lockers forward were water-logged. Since most of the trip had been made in that unbalanced condition, I guess we were lucky that they even made it. The children were bed-wetters and their mother no homemaker. Never before had we realized how really BIG a 54' boat is ... especially when it has been neglected and abused.

Since it was late evening, the "crew" asked if they could spend the night aboard ... they planned to rent a car for the return trip to Florida. We agreed. Another night could not make things any worse. The older couple had so enjoyed the trip; the children were untrained but innocent, we could not punish them for the untrustworthiness of their parents. With some effort we maintained our composure while we paid the last bills for the trip.

Hand in hand Joe and I wordlessly made our way back to our old car. Neither of us could say what was in our thoughts, so we were silent. Realizing that regret would be futile and counter-productive each of us thought only of doing what had to be done. We'd always managed before, hadn't we? That conspiracy of silence lasted for the five years we were to own the Nevins. Only later would we admit to each other how stricken we had been that night. Not that the boat was hopeless ... only that we had thought it would be so much better than it actually was, and indeed it had looked beautiful when Joe bought it. How quickly a poor skipper can destroy a ship.

The next morning when we got back to the boat everyone had departed. Joe and I rolled up our sleeves. Before, when we had gone to clean out previously owned boats we had used a big box; with this boat we needed to borrow our son Joey's landscaping truck.

Sloan had told in his book about installing the piano, bathtub and retractable table ... each project costing $1,000 or more ... but we found that most of the projects he had hired done at such expense actually detracted from the boat. The wood and plexiglass table blocked out the light from the hatch; raised and lowered by a pulley contrivance, it was unstable and out of character with the boat .. home it went. The bathtub was a cheap, six foot steel house tub which was mounted on a rude platform and took up the entire forecastle. It was brought to the dump and the whole forecastle gutted. The shipmate stove had been spray-painted red ... tacky and dirty ... UGH ... it too went to the dump. (We probably should have sand blasted it clean but that didn't occur to us till we started pricing a replacement.) The deckhouse cushions were old, faded and lumpy ... out. Window coverings were dust catching and not to our taste ... out. Redwood lawn furniture on the bridge deck ... inappropriate for a yacht ... take home. Air conditioners in the deckhouse and main cabin were rusty, dented and inappropriate; one worked and could be cleaned up for household use but the one above the galley had salt water damage and was caked with grease ... it went to the dump. Its wooden cover went home, since the marine plywood was salvageable.

The piano, which Sloan had paid $2,000 to install for his bride, posed the worst problem. None of us could play. It dominated the deckhouse, blocking the port windows and the hatches into the engine room, making furniture arrangement, cleaning and painting nearly impossible. The installation had been so costly because it had required opening the deck-house roof and hiring a crane to lower the piano into place. We could not afford to reverse that procedure. Joe said we would have to dismantle and remove it in pieces. In view of the prices old uprights fetch today, that was a regrettable but unavoidable solution. I had always dreamed of learning someday so I was not happy with the decision ... I had hoped Joe could work around the piano and save it for my retirement when I might still find time to learn ... but there was no way. I lost that one.

The night we destroyed the piano remains unforgettable. Most of the children were there to help. If you've never attacked a piano, you can't imagine how hard one is to kill. The musical screams echoed through the deserted boatyard till after midnight. We finally got down to the sounding board and struggled with it through the narrow deckhouse door and ashore.

PRETTY BETTY stood clean and empty ... ready for Joe to begin restoration. First, though, he went to New York and made arrangements to document the boat. Since I refused to change my name to Betty he changed the boat's name to LADY JEANNE.

Removal of the air conditioners had left the boat with two gaping holes, so we stayed on at the Greenport Yacht and Shipbuilding Co. and arranged for them to make a new hatch to replace the air conditioner over the galley and a jump window for the deckhouse. When we got the bill for that work (over $1,000) we realized that anything else we wanted done would have to be done by our own efforts. The cost of dockage also mounted quickly; we knew we had to get the boat to a mooring.

At that time the Shelter Island Yacht Club still rented moorings to non-members so we stayed on one of their moorings for the remainder of that season.

A family outing on PRETTY BETTY ... soon after purchase.

In spite of all the work we planned to do, we decided to get as much use out of the boat as possible. Joe cleaned and scrubbed, then made sure everything was safe so we could live aboard every weekend. Even though it was a half hour car ride, a ferry ride, and a ten minute walk to the Yacht Club we enjoyed keeping the boat on Shelter Island. We seldom took the car on the ferry since we had plenty of hands to carry supplies and the hike increased the aura of adventure. Walking over also prevented long waits at the ferry on busy summer weekends. When friends and relatives came to visit us the club's launch would bring them out and return them to shore when we signalled with three blasts on the horn. What luxury!

There was always work for foul days, but when it was fine we cruised. Around and around Shelter Island and into every delightful harbor. Once when all the children were with us we anchored in Cherry Harbor on Gardiners Island, then rowed to the north of the island where we swam in the most memorably cold and clean water. (The island is privately owned, so going ashore is verboten.) On long weekends we returned to Fishers Island and to Connecticut. We slipped up the Mystic River to enjoy the Seaport with its countless exhibits, now more pertinent since we owned our own "antique" boat. In spite of close quarters in the upper river, our 54' Nevins picked her way daintily, her twin screws and triple rudders enabling her to turn in her own length. After owning the Fletcher boat, which would skate around in the least breeze, it was a pleasure to wait for a bridge to open in a boat heavy and well-designed enough to stay put.

Wherever we went, our old princess elicited admiration. She looked so lovely slicing through the water. On every trip I would find an opportunity to lie on the forward deck and watch the bow wave curl back from her knife bow; her straight stem and perfect flare bespoke the sure eye of the master designer, George Mower. I never remember taking a wave over that competent bow.

In October when the yacht club closed up shop, we moved LADY JEANNE down to Larry's Lighthouse Marina in Aquebogue, just five miles away from our nursery-home, where, except for brief outings, she would remain for the next two years. There was so much to do, but the boat was basically sound. Nevins had built her with care using fine woods and bronze fastenings. During Sloan's ownership he had tried to keep up with necessary repairs and replacements. After his acquisition in 1966 at a cost of $18,000 he had installed a new 6.5 KW generator, keel bolts, shaft logs and strut planks, replaced bilge pumps and starting batteries, added an auto pilot, R D F radio and bow rail as well as the piano, fireplace, air conditioners and bathtub already mentioned. He had also just rebuilt the engines. There was still so much to do.

By this time, the day nursery encompassed three buildings and was busy enough to need Joe's full time help, so he could only put in about four hours of work on the boat every day sandwiched between two four-hour stretches of maintenance, repairs and cleaning at the nursery. One of the first major jobs he tackled was eliminating the big seat which had been built onto the foredeck. I don't know when this had been added, but it had never been properly bedded. It was completely water-logged and every screw which held it was admitting water into the cabin roof and onto the dining table. He also removed all the stanchions and rails since they were also causing leaks. It was really unfortunate that so many things had been improperly bedded on the deck; with proper care it would have still been sound with its heavy, imported canvas and sturdy felt paper laid over a teak base.

Joe was a very tidy worker who tackled one job after another and cleaned up every day. In spite of never-ending projects there was always some area of the boat kept cozy and liveable. During the years of work it was always a haven for both of us. Almost every day while the nursery children napped in the care of our fine staff, I would bring lunch down to the boat and Joe would stop to eat, talk, dream and listen to our favorite music.

With the charcoal fireplace radiating warmth as needed, we watched the seasons come and go in that protected tidal creek, in sight of an ever-changing marsh with its families of water birds. More than the restless pursuit of ever new destinations, that quiet companionship is for us the essence of the boat-owning experience.

Joe had wasted no time getting a good protective coat of paint on before winter and we had a cockpit cover, but snow storms were no fun. As soon as possible, often before the roads had been plowed, Joe would hurry to the marina to scoop and sweep the snow off the boat. He would start the engines and stir up the water in an effort to keep it from freezing in hard ... a field of slush around the hull prevented the gouging that so often results from skim ice. After three winters in wet storage our strong mahogany hull was unmarred, but he could never skip a below-freezing day. On one such stormy evening at low tide Joe slipped on the steep, icy ramp and cracked a rib. Months of discomfort followed.

The family in 1972.
Front, l to r: Elaine, Paul, Jeanne, Marie
Rear, l to r: Joe, Jeanne, Michele, Jim, Jeff, Joey and Renee

Wet storage during the winters is the best choice for large wooden boats; icy drying winds don't do wood hulls any good, but they should be hauled every year and allowed to dry for two weeks. Then, scraping and sanding should be followed by two coats of good anti-fouling paint. We had always done this with previous boats but only once did the Nevins get the full treatment. Once you get to a 54' boat you can't go to the small, inexpensive boatyards with the modest travel lifts. You have to depend on large commercial yards with marine railways ... and they have to do ALL the work. For example: haul and paint bottom ... $1,000 or more.

During the summers our son, Jim, was put on the payroll to help with the painting; somehow it seemed that we would never finish. The canvas on the huge foredeck needed replacement but we couldn't bring ourselves to invest that much more in a 50 year old boat. Joe worked valiantly but this time his perfectionism told against him. He was never satisfied with his results ... no matter how hard he tried he still had an OLD boat. She could be preserved, but doing the restoration correctly would cost more than we were willing to spend. Ownership of such a craft requires one of two kinds of owner: one with unlimited funds, or one who will settle for a comfortable old lady. We fit neither category.

Jeanne in the freshly painted galley of the Nevins. Ice box is across from galley. Door at right is to forecastle

Feeling a little guilty, like men who have grown tired of their wives, we started to look around. We realized that we would never be able to do justice to our old treasure and that as we grew older we would not need so much room. We could see that the aft cabin we had so desired would not be needed when the children were gone ... it was hard to heat and lonely back there. Our family had shrunk to a quiet threesome ... only Paul joining us most of the time. Michele was working toward her MBA at Harvard, Joey and Jeff were married, Renee working as a governess, Jim, Marie, Jeanne and Elaine were still in high school but they were all too busy with friends and work to think about cruising.

During the next months we would find that selling an OLD boat is even harder than buying one.

5

EGG HARBOR SEDAN
1971 37'

POOR RICHARD
(renamed LADY JEANNE)
Power: Palmer V8 265 h.p. twin gas

1974

Once you decide to sell a boat something vital goes out of your relationship to it. From being the repository of your dreams it suddenly becomes excess baggage. When you want to move on to new pastures the old dream must go; when you are dealing with a 50 year old 54' wooden cabin cruiser the accomplishment of that transition is likely to be filled with frustration and delay. We had thought that finding a good old boat was difficult; during two years we found that selling that "good old boat" was even more difficult. At first we tried to sell her ourselves, but no matter how we worded our ads they brought little response; we finally enlisted the services of yacht brokers and boat yards.

In the meantime the search was on for a new dream. Just as heroin addicts must have a fix, boat addicts must have a boat to love. We could not wait for the Nevins to be sold before starting the search for another boat. Since all our boat money was tied up in the Nevins we had to look for new money. We had bought our day care center before real estate prices had started to climb and the small, ten year mortgage was then half paid off. We were able to remortgage the then more valuable property for $30,000 at 8½ percent. That was the only time we came out ahead in a banking relationship: soon after negotiating that mortgage the money supply dried up and interest rates began their endless climb. With money in the bank we went shopping, ready to make that classic mistake: buy another boat before finding a buyer for the old one.

OLD boats were definitely out! We were finished with worn out knees and paint spattered clothes. No more aching backs for us ... but we still loved wooden boats. New boats were mostly fiberglass. What to do?

We began to look at Egg Harbors. We'd always admired them but they had been beyond our means. Though they, too, had begun production of glass boats, there were many wooden ones of recent vintage available and they were tempting. We began to follow them, visiting Connecticut and New Jersey boatyards and marinas where many were stored and used.

Egg Harbor had a fine reputation as far as we could discover. They advertised: " ... an extremely soft, dry ride ... responsive to the helm, surprisingly free of roll for a round bottom design ... they do not lift or plunge in choppy waters ... "

That sounded like just what we wanted: a beautiful boat, comfortable for life aboard combined with a hull design that would deliver a soft, dry ride. Their sportfishermen and express cruisers were in wide use off the New Jersey coast where they went out after big fish. We looked at several of these but, without exception, they had been abused. We were looking for one that had been treasured. The sedan models seemed more desirable with their enclosed salons and lavish use of varnished wood in cabinets and bulkheads. Models beginning as far back as 1963 were really fine, combining craftsmanship of pre-war years with modern styling and convenience.

By this time we were really intent on finding a boat that would be a very comfortable home for year-round living. Since some of our grown children were working in our day nursery we envisioned gradually turning the business over to them, as we took longer and longer vacations leading up to a fairly early retirement. We wanted to have our boat all ready when that day came.

By the fall of '74 the Nevins was still unsold, so we took her back to Larry's in Aquebogue while we kept on looking. In March '75 we found the POOR RICHARD in Connectiut's Yacht Haven West and we fell in love again. She was one of Egg Harbor's last wooden boats, 37' of beautiful wood work with lavishly upholstered convertible sofa, white leather chairs and plush red carpet in the salon, a modern galley with Princess electric stove and oven, full size 110 refrigerator powered by an Onan generator, full head with shower, plush dinette with drop-leaf formica table and another convertible sofa, as well as vee bunks forward.

She had every imaginable comfort and convenience topped off by a flying bridge and our first radar. Accustomed as we were to more spartan surroundings we were simply dazzled. Though we had always vowed "never again" to gas engines we silenced our misgivings on that score. Where would we ever find such a beauty again? The many positive features outweighed the disadvantage of her twin gas engines. Best of all, except for a good cleaning (her owner kept a cat aboard), she was ready to move into ... no more paint scraping ... the varnished interior was perfect. The crowning touch was a fine AM/FM radio with tape deck; after losing more than one portable radio overboard while trying to have constant music, who could resist? The deal was made.

We decided that this time we would really go "first class," start off with a new looking boat. We had the former owner deliver the boat to Essex Boat Works where we contracted for a full paint job to the outside. Determined to have everything perfect we also arranged to have fly bridge and cockpit enclosures made ... we were going to live aboard in COMFORT!

By the end of June all was ready. In spite of the new mortgage we had over-spent and borrowed more, but we had a real dream boat, so we were happy. We drove to Connecticut, parked our old car at the boatyard and started for home with our beautiful LADY JEANNE. That was our first ride in her.

It wasn't as soft and stable as we had hoped ... one of the engines was running poorly and we couldn't maintain the proper cruising speed ... Joe assured me that a "tune-up" would take care of everything. When we got home we refilled the gas tanks and were really surprised at how much the trip had cost ... those Palmers were surely thirsty. Well, the boat was mostly to live on, we just wouldn't overdo the long trips. We brushed aside one worry after another; the boat looked lovely.

We still had the Nevins stored at Larry's; he let us stay at an old bulkhead for a modest fee and Jimmy continued to work on her ... painting endlessly. We rented a slip at the Sterling Harbor Marina in Greenport, New York and made believe we were rich, plugged into shore power at a fancy marina, our new yacht right at home with the yachts of the rich and famous. We missed the privacy we had enjoyed at a mooring, but we were unwilling to listen to the generator for any length of time, and everything aboard depended on electricity: cooking, hot water, heat and refrigeration. Staying at a dock created a problem we had not anticipated: sometimes we would head out for a cruise on what seemed like a perfect day but the weather would often change at mid-day bringing gusty, gale force winds.It was hard to dock safely when that happened; we found ourselves looking for perfect forecasts before leaving. (You can always grab a mooring marker in the worst weather and safely wait out the storm before rowing ashore.)

When we did decide on a cruise we would have to worry about the budget; we could squeeze out the dockage but with gas prices continuing to climb our two big gas engines could consume our week's food budget in a few hours. In an effort to reduce the operating cost we tried to run at 10-12 knots, a solution that was successful with full displacement hulls but not workable with the wooden Egg. Designed to cruise at 18-20 knots she really was at the mercy of waves and wakes when we ran her so slowly. Neither of us got much of a tan that summer; we agreed that bathing suits were inappropriate in such a busy marina.

Before that summer was over we had to admit to each other that once again we had made a mistake ... this was not a boat with which we could happily spend the rest of our lives. People who enjoy cocktail parties and boat hopping combined with Sunday marina hopping adore Egg Harbors. That was just not our style.

Twice during that year we had to call a repairman to service the radar, an expense we resented. We had always been competent to repair most things and did not really enjoy having equipment beyond our skills. I never depended on the radar, anyway, I always dead-reckoned every course. The sliding windows which had looked so modern proved to be a source of trouble: the channels blocked up easily, allowing water to seep into trunk cabin and wheelhouse panelling. A spot which had looked like a knot in the wood of the wheelhouse turned out to be rot, it would need a new plank. Our marina's repair foreman estimated the cost of that at close to $1,000.

The port engine, which never did perform well, needed a valve job: estimate $550. In spite of the excellent, professional paint job the wood at the four corners of the flying bridge was beginning to rot ... it had not been properly bedded to the roof. The dacron and plexiglass bridge and cockpit enclosures were disappointing, requiring hours of care to remove salt and rapidly growing mildew. The shower, which had seemed like such a good feature, turned out to be a mess to use: the half hour needed to clean up the head after showering made bathing an unpleasant chore instead of a relaxing pleasure. Only a tub or a fully enclosed shower would solve that problem. Most people use a boat for perhaps ten weekends and a two week vacation, they would manage, - but we wanted to live aboard for most or all of the year. The drop leaf table turned out to be wobbly and hard to get around, and the galley, located in the passageway, blocked traffic. In order to keep the refrigerator cold enough the generator had to be set at "on-demand" and it would go on every few minutes. Every cup of coffee meant listening to the generator ... a price we were less and less willing to pay.

Paul on the deck of our Egg Harbor: Sterling Harbor Marina

We found we really could not live with the danger of fire or explosion and the high cost of operation and maintenance of our two big gas engines and gas generator. Most important of all, we missed the privacy of living on a mooring. This boat, like so many modern boats, required an umbilical cord to shore power. It was a lovely dockside motel ... not a self-sufficient sea going ship.

Egg Harbor was supposed to be one of the best ... and it was a very fine boat in many ways. If it could not suit us, where would we find a boat that could? Once again we surveyed the market. There did not seem to be any boat at any price that could satisfy every one of our very particular demands.

Our neighbors at that marina, George and Ruth Roth, took us for a day's outing on their LeComte, a 34' fiberglass sloop, and the pleasure of that cruise led us to explore the possibilities of sail. While we agreed that it was wonderful to listen to wind and water instead of big engines, we realized that we would require a larger sailing vessel than we could safely handle to encompass the comforts we wanted. Many of the sailing folk we talked to agreed that a power boat was preferable when looking toward retirement. Our lack of any experience with sail combined with the thought of cramped quarters, few creature comforts and the need for a crew when we so loved privacy ... all contributed to our decision to stick with power.

We had two big boats that we did not want to keep. We listed them with every broker and kept looking for a boating solution. If we could sell both boats at half-way reasonable prices we would be in a position to buy a really fine boat ... if we could find one. Boats were too much a part of our lives; we could not give up the search.

In May '75, one broker brought us a customer who seemed genuinely interested in the Nevins, to the point of having us haul the old girl for a survey. The survey was generally favorable, a contract was written, the broker accepted a downpayment and Joe spent a month getting things done on the boat to satisfy this potential buyer. The buyer ordered the yard to scrape and paint the bottom while the boat was hauled, even though the sale had not been completed. The boatyard complied and sent the buyer a bill for $1,000. We never saw that buyer again.

The broker's efforts to contact him only resulted in nasty letters from a New York law firm. The broker and the boatyard split the down-payment and we still had our boat. I guess if we'd hired a lawyer we could have enforced the contract, but we didn't want someone to buy the boat under duress. We loved our old ship too much, in spite of the fact that we couldn't keep her ourselves. We had given up our slip at Larry's and hauled at Greenport for the survey. What to do?

We thought we might have better luck selling if the boat was on a mooring in a busy harbor. Dering Harbor on Shelter was the scene of great summertime activity, so we bought a big mooring from Jack's Marine and had him install it on the shore opposite the yacht club. We posted big *FOR SALE* signs on port and starboard ... and hoped.

Soon after, the same broker brought us a couple of prospects for the

Egg Harbor but they also turned out to be duds. One, hearing that we had two boats to sell, assumed that we were desperate and made what had to be called an insulting offer. The other one wanted the bad spot in the wheelhouse fixed and the valve job done first, which was reasonable, but his offer wasn't. In spite of those two problems with the boat she was still the finest of her kind on the coast. (We knew that because we had looked at all of them.) We were not going to give her away.

We thought there would be a bigger market for the Egg Harbor on the south shore of Long Island, and remembered that broker Bennet Minton in Freeport had his own slips where he displayed a select assortment of quality boats for fussy buyers. We went to see him, showed him pictures of the boat, and honestly described her problems. He had a customer who was seriously looking for exactly what we had to sell. He said he would send two off-duty marine patrolmen to pick up the boat in Greenport and bring it to Freeport so no time would be lost. His customer loved the boat and Minton had the necessary repairs done in his own yard, charging us just what it cost him: $150 for the wheelhouse plank and $55 for the engine. Best of all, he got us a fair price. What a pleasure it was to do business with that honest man. Within a week we were down to one boat again. Of all the boats we have owned the Egg Harbor was the only one we sold with no feeling of nostalgia. She had been an expensive lesson but had never captured our hearts. Infatuation, not true love!

Since we already had the Nevins on our own mooring in Shelter Island we moved back in and really enjoyed living aboard her that year. Most of the time Joe and I went out to the boat alone. Though Paul was just ten he often preferred to stay with his older brothers and sisters at the nursery where there were lots of playmates, or to visit Joey and his wife, Nancy. After twenty-six years of child rearing we enjoyed the peace and quiet. Though we had been very protective of our children when they were small, we were willing to let them go as they sought independence, a non-interference policy we have not regretted. We had enjoyed our children but it was nice to have time for each other again. We had always known that the most important thing to save for your retirement is your marriage. We were still best friends.

We poked in and out of local harbors hoping someone would see our Nevins and want to own her. On one such foray into Sterling Harbor two men hailed us from a boat in the marina and made arrangements to look at the boat at her mooring. We crossed our fingers. They came and looked ... they liked the boat, but months would pass before they contacted us again.

In the meantime we continued our search ... at that point we had decided to look for a boat builder in Maine. The money from the Egg Harbor was drawing interest; if we could just sell the Nevins we could have a boat built to order.

We began to make regular trips to Maine looking for a builder; weekends in between were spent on the boat. As always, we hated to end the boating season ... that year it was November before we called it quits. Since our mooring was so far from the town dock it was often hard to get out to the boat. We finally broke down and bought an outboard motor for our dinghy, against our principles, we would much rather row. The motor didn't last long. Once we taught Paul how to run it he used every opportunity to cruise around the harbor. On one such outing the motor fell off, sputtering wildly as it sank to the bottom. We grappled, even sent a diver searching, but the engine eluded us. Back to the oars. One evening while attempting to row out to the boat we were blown to the far shore and had to tie the dinghy there and walk back to the ferry, abandoning all thought of our night aboard. We gave up. The next calm day we took the Nevins back to Larry's in Aquebogue.

We had just about despaired of hearing from our summer prospect when a phone call brought welcome news. The retired coast guardsman who had looked at the boat in the summer was ready to make an offer. He had sold his boat and would give us $12,000 for the Nevins. What a blow!

Always before when we had sold a boat we had come out almost even or ahead, because we had always improved the boat so much. We had certainly worked hard on the Nevins, and we knew she had many years of useful life ahead, but in two years this was only our second offer. Swallowing our disappointment we accepted. The buyer and his nephew planned to live aboard year round. During the nation's bi-centennial celebration the Nevins was used to ferry dignitaries around New York Harbor. When Guy Lombardo died the boat appeared on television as part of a tribute to the great band leader. On January 6, 1979, when we were on our way to live in Maine, we stopped in Cos Cob to see the old girl ... she looked great.

6

UHLRICHSON SEA SKIFF
1957 23'

ISHMAEL
Power: Palmer 160 h.p. gas

During the months while we had struggled to sell the Nevins and Egg Harbor we studied the available production boats, including trawlers and sailing vessels. Every one fell short in some way. We began to wonder if we could be satisfied. Everyone who vacations in Maine notices the countless lobster boats running the coast and plying the harbors; for landlubbers they are but a picturesque element of the area, but for boat lovers, they are much more. We noticed how smart and responsive these fishing boats are, how they set forth year round in all kinds of weather and usually return safely. After many Maine trips we became convinced that a pleasure cruiser based on the Maine lobster hull would provide a custom-made solution for us.

We visited boat builders in tiny Maine villages and observed them at work; they seemed to put out an honest product, but most of those who specialized in lobster boats were not eager to build for pleasure. Pleasure boating people tend to be a pain in the neck, always requiring special effects and tying up production. Boatbuilders get lots of visitors in their shore-side shops: tourists with time to kill who can spend all day shooting the breeze, wasting time and money for busy crews and owners. A serious, boat-buying customer has to try harder to get their attention. Even finding their shops is far from easy. They are unwilling to advertise their locations, and their signs are often small, faded, hand-lettered, and over-grown with weeds, or nailed to a tree or fence at a lonely intersection or driveway which always looks too private for a commercial establishment.

Having read about one of these elusive Maine builders you can leave the main highway early in the day, drive endlessly, ask directions often, and consider yourself lucky if you find him before dark. Once in the shop you can admire the hull under construction and describe your own needs, but persistent questioning will not elicit sample plans or hopeful suggestions. They usually say: "I'm all booked up for this year," or "Got lots of repair work to do after this, don't know when I'll be able to start another boat," or "My carpenter quit, so I'm goin' lobsterin'."

We finally found our builder through a combination of luck and dogged determination. One sunny day we left Rte. 1 in Orland to look for Joel White's boat shop in Brooklin. The roads on that Maine peninsula are narrow, twisting and seldom labeled. Well, there will be a sign at the intersection, but that will be the only one. After a half hour on a winding road you are no longer sure of where you are. We were sure we were lost and had pulled over by a vacant house to study our map. A jolly man stopped to see if we were interested in buying the house. We confided that our quest was in search of a boatbuilder ... not a house. Determined to be helpful, he said he knew just the man for us.

"Go see Bobby Rich down on Mount Desert Island ... he's the best boatbuilder and man you could hope to find!"

He was so enthusiastic that we took his advice, turned tail and plotted a course for Bernard, Maine. How fate intervenes ... it would be four years before we'd be back looking for Joel White once again.

When we found Bobby Rich's Bass Harbor Boat Shop he was working on a 46' lobster boat. He told us right off that he had two years of work piled up. That did not sound hopeful, but he didn't outright refuse to consider building for us, and, more important, he had built many pleasure boats so he knew what was involved. We were to visit that shop many more times before he agreed to build for us; when he finally drew us a set of plans we were overjoyed. We would have to wait, but it would be worth it to get a really fine custom-built Maine boat!

In the meantime we would have to buy a small boat to play with; we could not skip two seasons of boating ... NO WAY! In March and April we once again began to haunt boatyards ... this time, looking for something that ran and would float ...for a few hundred dollars. We dared not spend more, since we had reserved our place with Bobby Rich and had to save every dollar for the new boat.

We looked at every cheap sea skiff on Long Island. We wanted something with two bunks, a head, and an inboard engine ... those were our minimum requirements. Having a boat means being able to sleep aboard, anything else is not boating to us. Anyone who has tried to get a small sleep-aboard boat for a few hundred dollars knows what a challenge that is. Almost everything we went to look at was hopeless. We didn't expect much, but we certainly didn't want a complete rebuilding job on our hands, just something to keep us busy while our new boat was in the works.

Finally we found a 1957 23' Uhlrichson skiff in New Suffolk Shipyard.

Her name was ISHMAEL. She had been stored outside for a couple of years but the boatyard owner assured us that the fresh water cooled engine had been running when he had hauled it for storage. The owner had bought another boat and finally told the yard to sell, asking $500, just enough to settle storage bills. He accepted our offer of $450.

Sadly neglected, with a broken window in the shelter cabin, full of debris, ISHMAEL was still basically sound. Her mahogany lapstrake planks and oak frames were dried out, but not rotten, her rivets still mostly holding. She had vee bunks and a head, as well as a wood shelter top. She would do.

Joe swung into action. Out with the junk. Scrape the bilges. Dig out the rot. Scrape old paint. He gathered up all his old, odd, bronze screws and bolts and went over the hull, refastening every plank that was not holding tight. He dug out dried seam compound and sister-ribbed a couple of cracked ribs. Then he replaced the dirty old head with a compact, new model (how many heads have we bought?) and ordered a new glass for the shelter top. He removed a pailful of old wires and cleaned up the engine. We had a canvas man measure and fit a new cockpit cover to protect the boat when we left it, as well as three drop curtains with plexiglass windows to drop from the shelter roof to the engine box and deck. These would make it possible to enjoy cruising in the autumn ... our favorite time on the water. During that year (1975) I was taking some child development courses at Empire State College in Westbury, so while Joe was scraping and painting I kept him company, sharing new learnings with him.

The work we did on ISHMAEL is described in a few sentences; but it was actually late in July before everything was done. By the time we were ready, everyone else had been launched.

In May, we took time out to go to Michele's wedding. She and Per Sorensen had met when he was rowing on the Charles River in Boston; they were both working on their MBA degrees, he at Sloan, she at Harvard. After the simple reception at the Harvard Faculty Club, son Joey and his wife Nancy took Paul home with them, and Joe and I had a lovely 28th wedding anniversary vacation ... alone in Maine. Then, back to work.

Since the boat had been out of water for over two years we launched very cautiously, lowering into the water but keeping it suspended in the travel lift in case we couldn't keep up with the leaks. We knew it would take time for the planks to swell. We moved aboard with pumps and buckets on Friday afternoon, determined to stay with ISHMAEL until she was seaworthy. Our concern proved to be well founded. The water rushed in. We pumped and bailed well into the night, taking turns trying to grab some sleep. By morning, the flood began to abate. We spent the remainder of that weekend reading, boat still in sling, making sure the automatic bilge pump we had installed could handle the influx.

By Monday morning we could move to a slip, fasten the cockpit cover and go back to work, asking the yard to call us if the boat looked low in the water. We had never stayed at this boatyard-marina before, but we had so enjoyed being there while working on the boat that we rented a slip for the rest of the season. It was located in a quiet, little creek with over-hanging trees, marshy wet lands and lots of birds.

Joe had replaced points and plugs on the six cylinder valve-in-head Palmer marine engine, cleaned the carbuerator, drained the old gas, oil, and anti-freeze in the fresh water cooling system and bought a new, heavy-duty Mopar battery. With a couple of shots of ether the engine turned over and after some initial sputtering it ran quite well. We were thankful since we realized that the engine could as well have been a total loss ... it was a chance ... and we won.

During the remainder of that season, and until our Rich boat was launched, Joe and I had as much enjoyment out of that cheap, old boat as we have had out of any boat. We realized then that while we liked to have a beautiful boat we could be happy as long as we could be on the water in a safe, clean boat ... no matter how small! Two bunks and a head, camp stove and picnic cooler, warm sleeping bags and no leaks in the top-sides ... heaven!

We really didn't trust that little, old boat and old engine for extensive cruises but, based on beautiful Peconic Bay, we had lots of interesting, short-haul cruising at our doorstep. The long cruises would come when the Rich boat was ready; we were content to putter around Long Island's bays.

ISHMAEL, after renovation, in her slip in New Suffolk

After living aboard large cabin cruisers for so many years we found living aboard a sea-skiff required careful planning and use of space, but it was a picnic preparing for two people after all the years with eleven! We bought two string hammocks to hang above our bunks; each of these held a complete change of clothes (always mandatory in case someone falls over-board), warm sweat shirts, and swim suits rolled into beach towels for swimming and sunbathing. A plastic bin with a handle contained all necessary toiletries: shaving, grooming and first aid supplies. We put a hook above the windshield so we could hang a mirror at the right height for shaving. A plastic wash basin hung on the port side of the shelter cabin was used just for bathing, and a good sized towel rod for light-weight towels and wash cloths completed our grooming area ... yes, you can keep clean in a small boat!

Joe built a shelf along the starboard side of the helm area to form a galley counter. In it he installed a small, rectangular stainless steel sink with an outboard drain so we could wash our few dishes. Dishes and utensils fit in a plastic bin which was stowed right above the mini-galley. We had a small, one-burner Coleman camp stove which fit easily on the shelf, leaving some space for food preparation. The engine box made a roomy table, we each had a folding helm seat ... we were as comfortable as could be. We carried a five gallon jug of water, as well as a smaller jug which was easier for me to lift. Had we kept the boat another season we would have installed a water tank and pump.

With such a simple galley I found it most sensible to plan one-pot meals. Whenever I made such meals at home I would prepare and freeze some extra in containers which fit snugly in my cooler. When the weekend rolled around I would pack the cooler: two or three frozen main meals, a half-gallon milk carton of ice, eggs, milk, juice, sandwich fixings, fresh fruit and salad makings. Bread, crackers, home-made cake or cookies, bran flakes and raisins would complete the provisioning. (We consider the bran cereal a must when living aboard ... aid to regularity.) Coffee, tea, iced tea mix, sugar, coffee creamer and powdered milk were always kept aboard in quantity. Beer and soda drinkers need another cooler just for those beverages, but we had resisted becoming addicted to them; with nine children to feed we could not waste money on expensive treats so lacking in food value. Now that we have only ourselves to worry about we have relaxed enough to share a beer, but soda has no place in our diet.

Early in our cruising life I decided that keeping fresh meat on boats is a risky proposition. When I buy meat while cruising we always cook and eat it immediately. When we bring meat from home, it is already cooked: baked or fried chicken, small meat balls, or sliced roast can be heated quickly in beef or chicken bouillon and served with instant rice or Chinese noodles (these cook in three minutes). Add stir-fried vegetables or a salad, bread, simple dessert and coffee for a most satisfying meal.

On August 12, 1976, Hurricane "Belle" ripped through Suffolk County felling hundreds of trees; as always in a storm, we were aboard protecting our ship. We had rushed out to New Suffolk in advance of the storm to double up the lines and make sure the fenders were positioned advantageously. Expecting that high tides would raise the boat above the dock we also secured to trees on shore. Then we crawled into our bunks to await developments. The fixed dock was soon buried beneath foaming waves, branches were ripped from overhanging trees, wind whistled through the rigging of neighboring sailboats. Huddled in our rocking bunks sleep was impossible, still we felt better being there rather than at home worrying about ISHMAEL.

As we drove home the next morning we could see why eastern Suffolk had been declared a disaster area: trees down and detours everywhere. Family and staff at the nursery were relieved to see us home safe; sometimes they must have thought we were a bit nutty! Are other boat owners as compulsive?

During that year one of children ran afoul of the law: picked up with a pot-carrying friend, our youngster was arrested ... bail money, lawyer's bills, sorrow and humiliation followed. Did any parents of this generation escape?

In September Jeanne was married to Chris Young; since they had embraced the Hebrew-Christian faith they had a "Fiddler on the Roof" wedding .. canopy and mazeltov ... and oh the dancing! What fun. In October Jimmy took beautiful Gail Wilson to the alter. Three weddings in just over four months. Five of our children married, our first grandson thriving, (Joey's Jason b. 12-11-75), day care center expanding yearly, keel-laying for the new boat scheduled for January '77. We had never had such a busy year, but then, they had always been busy. Perhaps we tried to do too much ... Joe, almost fifty, was feeling the strain.

One weekend we found our old Elco abandoned in a boat yard near Threemile Harbor. That day seemed to mark a turning point for him; he came home sadly depressed at this dismal sight. Soon after, his mother died suddenly and tragically. Joe descended into a depression that no amount of reasoning could alter. Unable to concentrate on his usual succession of projects, our life together centered on our times alone on the little boat. It didn't seem to matter if we cruised ... we took long walks together trying to ease the pressure, hoping Joe would soon shake off the shadow on his spirit.

Paul visiting us on ISHMAEL in winter 1976

We extended our weekends, beginning them after lunch on Friday so we could get out to New Suffolk before the weekend traffic. At that point only Elaine and Paul were still at home. Having grown up in the nursery, Elaine at seventeen was a fine mother-substitute and eleven year old Paul's very good friend. They learned to help and support each other during our ever-increasing absences.

In November, realizing that the New Suffolk Marina was ill-equipped for winter ice, we rented a slip at the Sterling Harbor Marina in Greenport where we had lived it up in our Egg Harbor; they had a good bubble system and adequate electricity. With our canvas cover securely battened against the wind and our Aladin "blue flame" heater glowing, we continued to spend long weekends aboard during much of that winter. Of course, we turned off the Aladin when we went to sleep, leaving an electric heater on to keep us from freezing. We were thankful for the fresh water cooling system on the boat; with adequate anti-freeze we could operate all winter ... on eastern Long Island there are often winter days that cry out for a boat ride.

With the boat safe, we took a trip to Maine to see Bobby Rich. The 671 GM Diesel engine we had ordered for the new boat had been delivered, as well as the oak and mahogany for the hull. Right after New Year's Day the keel was laid and by the time we visited again in February the hull was all planked. The Rich boat would not be ready till June but we would not miss any part of a boating season. On April 1, we moved ISHMAEL to our mooring in Shelter Island where we continued to weekend until the new boat was ready.

Joe was still operating under a cloud ... unsure of the wisdom of building a boat while he felt so depressed. I hoped his depression would soon pass and, realizing how much boats meant to him, I encouraged him to continue to plan for the future. I did not want him to give up his dream.

Once the Rich boat was finished we decided to sell ISHMAEL, although it was with great regret. Had Joe felt better, we would have kept her; she was a fine little ship and we loved her. She had seen us through some rough days in our life together.

In July we sold ISHMAEL to a doctor who wanted to take his two young sons fishing around Shelter Island. We hoped they would be kind to her.

A couple of years later while walking on Shelter Island we found our little Uhlrichson Sea Skiff, still bearing the same name, tied to a dock in an almost deserted boat yard. We crept shyly aboard for a brief visit. Debris littered every inch of the cockpit; the new canvas we had so proudly installed was now lying crumpled and dirty in the cluttered cuddy cabin. How fleeting are our footsteps in life's sands. No trace remained of our loving care. ISHMAEL was doomed. Another sad farewell to a sweet dream.

"Call me Ishmael. Some years ago--never mind how long precisely--having little or no money in my purse, and nothing particular to interest me on shore, I thought I would sail about a little and see the watery part of the world."

The beginning of MOBY DICK by Herman Melville.

7

ROBERT F. RICH
DOWNEAST CRUISER
1977 43′

"LADY JEANNE"
Power: General Motors 671 260 h.p. diesel

Dear Bobby Rich. What a special place he had in our lives for so long. From the day when we found his shop in Bernard until the day in April '77 when he launched our LADY JEANNE, we must have visited him fifty times. We watched him build four boats while we waited our turn. Every time we could put three days together, we'd descend upon him. I wonder what he thought of us, in our beaten up old red Ford. He was used to building "summer" boats for rich folks, which we obviously were not. When we showed him pictures of our Nevins and Egg Harbor, both then desperately "for sale," I guess he realized we had the means to build a boat, which seemed unlikely if one just judged by our car.

Over those years I grew to think of him almost as of a father; I'd lost my own carpenter-father when I was thirteen, and there was a void in my life that Bobby filled. When we ran down the hill to his shop his "Hi Jeanie, Joe" accompanied by a hug and kiss for me and a hearty handshake for Joe made us feel like coming home.

The sawdust and wood shavings, the hulls which gradually took shape under his hands, the way he listened, head cocked, while we told him our ideas and he puffed away like a chimney, one cigarette after another; all impressions coalesced into an unforgettable experience.

Bobby loved the ducks which inhabit the Bass Harbor marshes and over the years he secured quite a following. He kept a bag of grain inside the shop door and every day at 4:30, after the men were gone, the local mallard population would assemble in confident expectation of the largesse he unfailingly scattered near the ways. He had no use for gulls and turtles who regularly dine on ducklings; he would sorrowfully note the gradual reduction of each brood because of these predators.

Our visits were usually made on the weekends when the big wood stove in the shop was cold so, after tramping around the work in progress till we were frozen, we'd go up to the house and Mildred, Bob's dear wife, would make us coffee. Then we'd debate all the fine points of boat construction; Bobby would recount his adventures with boats and customers. We were in boat lover's heaven.

During the summer of 1981 Bobby died of lung cancer (as I had feared he would) after a long illness. He was only 67 ... a strong and vital man who, in his life, had built close to two hundred honest boats. He was the son of a boat-builder, brother of two more, Roger and Ronald, and father of Chummy (Robert, Jr.) and Walter who carry on his traditions in the shop where we grew to know him so well. He is sadly missed here on Mount Desert Island. Though I was just on the fringe of his life, I miss him, too. I will always be proud of the lovely boat he built for us.

When we made the deal with Bobby to build for us, there was no such thing as a contract, only a handshake. The terms were established verbally: labor at $8.50 per hour, material at cost plus twenty percent markup. He would secure builders' risk insurance for which we would reimburse him ($455), and we would give him enough money each month to pay the bills. All bills were to be paid in full before delivery. Simple enough. There was never any problem. By the time the boat was finished there were 3,674 hours of labor in her ($31,235), materials valued at $30,636 and equipment, upholstery, plumbing, etc. in the amount of $4,263, plus the engine at $11,500 for a total cost of $77,633. Today, that same boat would cost at least twice as much to build.

When we began the planning for the Rich boat we set out to build a vessel on which two people could live year round in comfort. At this point it was obvious that our children would no longer cruise regularly with us; they were all too involved in work, studies and friendships, or in establishing their own families. Time for shifting gears.

The plan we evolved was based on one of Bobby's lobster hulls: 43' in length with a beam of 13'6". The layout from bow to stern included a rope locker and oil burner in the bow section, followed by a big bathroom (head) with built-in bathtub. Then to port, a galley, and to starboard a dinette which could seat four (rather snugly). Next, to port and starboard, two large pilot berths (6'6" x 30") with real innerspring mattresses. In front of and about a foot below each berth there was a settee and end table with drawer and an elegant reading lamp ... so cozy!

Three steps led to the wheelhouse where two sturdy and attractive Pompanette helm chairs were securely fastened to the deck. Big hatches opened for servicing the 671 General Motors Diesel engine. Canvas curtains, removable for hot weather, enclosed the wheelhouse. The big aft cockpit was still large enough for dancing!

Our plans did not call for a generator. All of our experiences with that animal had been negative. Our Nevins and Egg Harbor had both had generators, so we'd had ample opportunity to assess the pros and cons. They are supposed to provide all the comforts of home, but just as a power failure leaves homes helpless, so does failure of a generator leave boat owners helpless. Heat, hot water, cooking, lights and refrigeration are all dependent on the almost constant barking of a very noisy motor. In our past experience the generators had been the most frequently troublesome; their repair required the service of experts, not always available and always expensive. I did not want another one.

Here, however, we ran up against a stubborn Bobby who insisted: "All pleasure boats have generators. A diesel generator will be trouble-free. I'll insulate it real good so the noise won't bother ... " The argument ground on and on. We were finally persuaded that it made good sense to have a generator; why risk the dangers of gas stoves and water heaters when electric stoves were so clean and safe? I have always preferred gas stoves, but I lost that one.

After all the years of painting boats, Joe was tired of painting. He wanted to have a varnished interior on this boat. He likes to varnish: so much less dust, no paint chips, no cracks when the boat works. We went to look at some lobster boats which had been varnished inside and we thought they looked great, but here again Bobby was adamant: "Fish boats are varnished; pleasure boats are painted white." He finally convinced us.

Recalling those debates I wonder if Bobby was just trying to save us money ... he knew that before varnish can be used on a pleasure boat wood grains must be matched and cuts made perfectly ... all time consuming; with paint, grains don't matter and wood dough covers mistakes.

Typical of Maine men who have grown up with hard times, Bobby was always thrifty; he just couldn't see the need of Bryunzeel plywood for the bulkheads. The Clayton Fletcher boat had bulkheads of exterior grade plywood which did not want to hold paint ... they needed constant care, while Bryunzeel holds any finish beautifully and never seems to rot. Even at almost one hundred-fifty dollars a sheet, we felt it was worth it. We won on this one.

We wanted a dry exhaust. He was horrified! He just wouldn't do it ... "only fish boats have dry exhausts." That was why we wanted one ... fish boats go out all year! I had also wanted insulated glass in the wheelhouse, but he could think of no possible way to install it.

As in all human relationships we found there was a lot of give and take involved in the process of building a boat. We were determined to have the very best materials. Bobby was sure some less fine would do just as well and save us money. (He knew we were not loaded!) Through long years of caring for boats we had come to realize that half the cost of building a boat is in material. Using the very best only adds ten to twenty percent to that cost.

Once a boat is built you can't change defective plywood or cheap fastenings, and the savings on repairs far outweigh the original investment.

In our own way we were as stubborn as Bobby. I'm sure he must have complained bitterly about how fussy we were, though he never let on to me. He was always chivalrous and kind to me and, I guess, to all women. I know that one time he ruined the lines of a boat because the stately lady had insisted on 7' headroom in the cabin. He could be gruff in dealing with men. Thus, it was always my portion to give him any bad news and, like daughters since time began, I would get around him, kid him and make him laugh and sometimes get my own way. The most important change I had to insist on his making involved the wheelhouse roof. When we arrived for one of our regular visits, the first thing that struck our eyes was the angle of the shelter top. It just looked wrong. When I showed Bobby and drew him a sketch of what I wanted, I could see that he was fit to be tied. He would have to take out a day's work to do it our way, but he did it. I know the boat was so beautiful because the roof line was exactly correct in relation to the hull line. A mistake here is fatal.

Bobby and Joe pose for me in front of our engine and a load of oak.
Grace Babcock's house is behind the fence.

When we had planned the boat we had wanted a cedar hull. Cedar is more resistant to rot, lighter, and tougher; it tends to spring back when dented. Unfortunately, the year we built there did not seem to be any good cedar coming out of the mills. Bobby said he rejected a couple of loads and then got a good load of mahogany. We ended up with a mahogany hull.

Lots of Bobby's pleasure boats had been finished with varnished trunk cabins and sterns. We had discovered that only paint protects wood adequately on the outside of a boat. As Bobby finished stern and trunk cabin he put off painting them, calling our attention to the lovely grain, hoping we would succumb to the beautiful wood and tell him to varnish them. We would agree that the wood was lovely and then close our eyes and say:

"PAINT"

Poor Bobby. We went against so many of his conventions. Imagine painting that precious mahogany!

When the boat was done she looked like a classy lobster boat, which was exactly what we had envisioned. We did not want a cabin cruiser with a Maine look. We wanted a finely built lobster boat designed for pleasure. Something genuine in a plastic world. That is what Bobby gave us. Every time we pulled into a dock with that vessel a crowd of boat lovers gathered to admire her.

During all the months of planning and building Joe grew more and more anxious. He slept poorly, felt depressed, and was easily upset. He seemed consumed by some nameless dread. I hoped that once the boat was finished he would be able to relax, get away from everything and feel like his old confident self again. The trips to Maine, once so gay and exciting, became grueling tests of endurance. As the date for launching drew near, Joe grew more and more nervous. He finally decided that the boat would have to be launched without the owners' presence. I was crushed. Another Jeanne, Bobby's bookkeeper, did the honors with the champagne bottle in my stead; the boat was lowered and the sea trials confirmed our highest hopes ... she handled beautifully!

We arrived a few days later and Bobby took us for our first ride in LADY JEANNE, and for our first view of Mount Desert Island from the sea. Across Bass Harbor bar with its striking lighthouse set against pink granite cliffs, along Seawall with its oft flooded causeway to Manset, through Western Way, Great Cranberry Island to starboard, we sped, and into the mountain fastness of Northeast Harbor, summer hideaway of the most discriminating nature lovers, many, rich and famous. The beautiful old seven inch compass which we had salvaged from the Nevins checked out perfectly on every course, and the LADY JEANNE performed just as we had hoped she would. Moving effortlessly, she cruised at 12 knots with an engine speed of 1850 rpm. We were delighted.

We made arrangements with Grace Babcock, a neighbor of Bob's who was also a fine seamstress, to make the canvas curtains for the wheelhouse, as well as jaunty curtains for the trunk cabin portholes to match the bunk covers she had already made. We invited Bobby to make the trip to Long Island with us; boat builders don't often get an opportunity to cruise in the beautiful boats they build, and we were somewhat fearful of making the trip alone, since we had always cruised in protected, inland waters before. Bobby's ready assent was really welcome.

We made plans to leave for New York on Friday, May 28th, weather permitting; if all went well we would arrive home on May 30th: our 29th wedding anniversary! Joe and I had long since ceased exchanging gifts, our boats kept us too poor, but what an anniversary gift that was!

There was not a ripple on the water in Bass Harbor when the sun cleared the horizon on the 28th. The most memorable cruise of our lives began at 5:30 A.M. Joe had the engine warmed up already when Bobby swung down the ramp, east off the docklines, and leapt aboard to take the helm. The one condition Bobby had made for the trip was that he run the boat. He was just too restless to sit around all day! The only time he left the helm was to hit the head, and that was seldom. Joe admired his endurance, considering how many cups of tea he put down each day.

Our first day's run took us to South Portland, 102 miles of the most beautiful real estate in the world. My yacht log and photo album confirm my memories: Bass Harbor, Casco Passage, Deer Island Thoroughfare, Fisherman Island Passage, Muscle Ridge Channel, Whitehead Island, Webster Rock and Cushing Island in Casco Bay were all beautiful beyond description. We were awestruck by the loveliness of the Maine coast. That day we vowed that Portland, Maine would one day be the western border of our world.

As the day wore on the wind gusted to a good 30 knots, as the white caps and blown hair in our pictures attest. Bobby kept the engine running at a steady 1850 rpm which delivered a reliable 12 knots; long before we reached Portland the spray was flying over the whole boat; the windshield wipers beat a path through the wall of water while I watched anxiously for every buoy. Had we been alone we would have slowed down, but Bobby was fearless, sure of his creation's competence in the sea.

As the lady of the "house" and navigator, I was kept mighty busy. Bobby smoked about five packs a day, so I found keeping his ashtray empty, matches handy, and ashes swept up almost a full time occupation. He enjoyed frequent tea breaks, but he was easy to feed: scrambled eggs, hot dogs and beans ... whatever I served was enjoyed and appreciated. He was even comfortable enough with us to put his store teeth in his pocket.

My skill as navigator was honed under Bobby's watchful eye. He would double check every course I drew, so I got in the habit of checking several times before presenting him with the next chart. He held the boat at such a constant speed that it was easy to predict time of arrival at the next buoy. We altered our course at Webster Rock because the seas were becoming too rough even for Bobby. Taking a more protected course around Cushing Island, we soon pulled into Marine East in South Portland. Not quite eight hours running time from Bass Harbor and with twelve hours on the engine, we had used 80 gallons of fuel at a cost of $38.54. The good old days!

We had persuaded son Paul, then twelve years old, to make the trip with us. feeling that it was too valuable an experience for him to miss ... and today he remembers it fondly and is glad he went ... but he was a somewhat disgruntled traveling companion. Since he had been refusing to cruise with us for several years, we had designed the boat to sleep two in comfort. Paul and Bob had folding cots in the wheelhouse. While Bobby insisted he could sleep on a rock, Paul was less agreeable. Complain, complain ... even pre-teens do that well; we vowed that if ever we built again we'd include guest berthing even if it was never used.

Bobby had many friends at Marine East; he had built a Penobscot design trawler for owner John McCarty during the winter before our boat was built. We had watched the building of that vessel more closely than John had, and had many pictures of her during construction. Our stay there was very sociable; we celebrated by going to dinner at the Bridgeway Restaurant which was just a short walk from the shore.

While our first day's run had taken us 102 miles, the second day promised to be even more; we set our sights on Onset, near the Cape Cod Canal.

The day dawned clear and still. We left Portland at 5:05 A.M., rounded Adams Head at 6:02 and took an offshore course of 236° for the "WI" whistle off Wood Island which we reached on schedule at 6:35 A.M. We altered course slightly to 232° and passed the "CP" whistle off Cape Porpoise at 7:19. Running the offshore buoys proved to be duck soup on a bright, clear day, but the next course to York Ledge would be seventeen miles, the wind picked up and the spray swept over us, the sky became overcast. Not so easy, now. I spent the time scanning the horizon hopefully, hanging on for dear life in the steep seas, trying to focus the binoculars, hoping to see the next buoy. On a heading of 223° we reached York Ledge at 8:51 A.M.; a hard buoy to find in the increasing chop. Our next course: 194° took us outside the Isle of Shoals right into the Bigelow Bight, 24 miles of ocean to the Dry Salvages off Cape Ann, which we rounded at 10:55. Still morning, and we had come so far. My confidence grew, in Bobby, boat, and compass, as well as my own skill as navigator. The longest run was still ahead: 32 miles across Massachusetts Bay to Farnham Rock. It was a relief to reach the relative calm of Cape Cod Bay. At 3:35 P.M. we reduced speed for the Cape Cod Canal, at 4:40 we reached the Onset Bay Channel and at 4:50 we tied to a fuel dock at Onset Marine. We had come 140 miles and used 76 gallons of fuel. It had been a long, hard day. We were all exhausted. After a simple supper we all fell into bed. Bobby promised us an early start.

True to his word, Bobby had us cast off at 5:30 A.M. on another incredibly beautiful clear day. It was Memorial Day and our twenty-ninth wedding anniversary. Once underway I went below to fix breakfast. The generator could not be heard above the steady thumping of the Jimmy diesel, so I enjoyed cooking on my beautiful Princess electric stove. Everyone also appreciated the luxury of real toast: one positive reward for the troubles with generators.

As soon as we cleared Onset Channel Bobby pushed the engine up to 1800 for the slide down Buzzards Bay; in spite of gusty winds we made 11.5 knots until we reached Point Judith at 9:50. We were halfway home. The seas worsened; Bob reduced throttle. Down the center of Block Island Sound we bounced 16.5 nautical miles to the "MOA" whistle, tricky to find, and 13 more to Constellation Rock. With the reduction in speed I was quite anxious before we sighted this buoy. It should be much bigger and higher. We plunged into treacherously steeper seas and, in surprise, Bobby reduced speed to 1300. He had often wondered why we wanted such a good "sea boat" since we cruised mostly inland waters, but the "inland waters" of Block Island and Long Island Sounds, Gardiners and Peconic Bays are often rougher and more dangerous than the Maine coast. In Maine, if you take offshore courses away from rocks and shoals, it's often more comfortable, since the water is deep, the waves farther apart. Maine is less forgiving, however, since the water is so frigid; if you make a stupid mistake and get wrecked you only have a few minutes before perishing unless you are wearing a perfect survival suit.

Past Plum Island and Orient Point, the waves diminished, we went around Hay Point and into Dering Harbor for journey's end. We picked up our mooring, and for the first and only time in all our cruising Joe left the boat without washing her down. He knew Bobby would be restless from all the hours at the helm, and it was our anniversary. The day was not over yet!

We rowed ashore, walked to the Shelter Island Ferry and crossed to Greenport where we found our old car, unmolested and still functioning, then drove the twenty miles to Riverhead for a happy homecoming.

Elaine had a festive anniversary dinner ready and we spent the evening recounting our adventures and enjoying Bob's inexhaustible store of boating anecdotes. The next day Joe and I took Bobby to MacArthurs Airport. Tearfully, I bade him goodbye, feeling as though one of the most memorable chapters in our lives was ending. It seemed to me that nothing could equal the excitement and anticipation we had experienced planning and building this beautiful boat and bringing her home.

We dug into the piled-up work at our day nursery. Our staff was quite accustomed to managing things in our absence but every time we came back there was the extra cleaning and bookkeeping, regrading of driveway and pruning of bushes awaiting us. The customers always knew when "Daddy" Merkel was home: everything took on a shine no one else could manage.

We took all our grown children, their friends and in-laws for day cruises on LADY JEANNE. They all agreed that she was beautiful.

Toward the end of June the generator failed: two bolts on the starter motor had broken off. We were powerless! We motored around Shelter Island to Coecles Harbor where there was a diesel mechanic who replaced the bolts. We also had this yard give the inside of the wheelhouse another coat of white paint. Though we only had 41 hours on the engine, Joe ordered an oil change. He was still quite anxious and compulsive about having everything on the boat perfect. The failure of the generator plunged him into gloomy thoughts.

After seemingly endless weeks of hard work at the nursery and Joe's increasing depression, I longed for escape. I started to plan another trip to Maine. I thought we would be wise to retrace our route during the same year and thus take advantage of the confidence and expertise we had gained on the trip with Bobby, consolidate our gains. Reasoning aside, I was tired of working and worrying about Joe; I wanted to go back to Maine!

On July 10th Michele's first child and our second grandchild, Peter, was born. Mother and baby were doing fine. I insisted that Joe go to see a family doctor as there seemed to be no reason why he should feel so blue.

What could be wrong? The doctor gave him a complete check-up and pronounced Joe to be an extremely healthy man; though 51 years of age, he had the body of a lad in his twenties. The doctor prescribed a mild anti-depressant. Joe took a few doses, but could not tolerate the side effects. When we were home we lived above the nursery, so there was always work waiting to be done. In Joe's mental state he was sleeping poorly and staying up later and later, working till midnight, and still unsatisfied with the day's accomplishments. I grew more and more tired. How I longed for the spruce clad islands and mountains, almost black against a sky rivaled only by my babies' blue eyes; how jealous I was of the folk who were feasting on the glory of Maine's wildflowers in summer. I counted the hours till we could escape from all the work and worry.

DERING HARBOR to BASS HARBOR ... July 1977

On July 23rd at 8:45 A.M. we dropped our mooring in Dering Harbor and began our second coastal cruise. This time we would take three weeks instead of three days; we would have time to see something, instead of always being under pressure. Once again son Paul agreed to accompany us.

As before, we planned to make Onset in one day. Our first courses repeated those we had taken with Bobby; we reached Point Judith's R "4" bell at 12:35 P.M. and Sakonnet Point at 1:05, but, by then, the waves were steeper. We made a foolish mistake. Instead of staying in deep water as we had before, we became frightened and took a heading closer to land. Our new course was for the black can C "1" off the Hens and Chickens: a reef consisting of many large boulders in two large groups, some of them awash only one foot or less. Close by is OLD COCK, a rock awash, marked by a day beacon and a sunken wreck (or wrecks, I should think). There are five buoys, all difficult to identify in a heavy sea, and the water shoals so that the heavy seas that day became steeper. All at once we were in the midst of that turbulent witch's cauldron, unable to read the buoys and afraid to go in any direction. Waves were breaking all around us. At any second we expected to hear the heart-stopping crash of hull against rock. Eyes glued to depth sounder and compass, we oozed our way into deeper water toward red gong "5" on Mishaum Ledge.

We learned a lesson that day. A chart is not enough help for cruising the coast; you must have dangers explained. At the first opportunity I bought the two U. S. Coast Pilots for our cruising area: #1, EASTPORT to CAPE CODE and #2, CAPE COD to SANDY HOOK. With Coast Pilot in hand I have learned to study each chart and put a big XX on any area described as dangerous, or requiring local knowledge. Local knowledge is hard to come by!

Subdued after our close call, we passed Fl G "1" at Wilbur Point, the "11" bell off Cleveland Ledge and, following the well buoyed channel to the steel dolphin "11" which marked the entrance to Onset Bay, we made it safely to Onset at 5:20 P.M. We filled the fuel tanks: 74 gallons for the 100 miles we had covered. Joe washed the boat, and we took a mooring for the night. Then we took to the dinghy and explored the harbor past Wickets Island to the town dock, where we tied the dink and went exploring the town. This is a lively resort town where stores and restaurants are plentiful. We rowed back to the boat in darkness, fighting off mosquitos, and scurried into our screened comfort to make dinner and plan for the next day.

We wanted to reach Portland, so we rose with the sun, cast off at 5:45 A.M. and ate breakfast while underway. We were not going to take any chances; we stuck with the tried and true courses we had taken with Bobby. The weather held clear and we reached Portland at 6:30 P.M. after an uneventful but tiring passage. We filled fuel and water tanks and took a berth for the night. That evening we explored South Portland, getting needed exercise and discovering the services that would have been available had we arrived earlier.

The next morning we cast off at 7:00 A.M. and took the Diamond Island Roads and Whitehead Passage into Casco Bay, but we did not get far. What had been a moderate breeze in South Portland developed into a moderate gale in the open coastal waters. We climbed a few mountainous waves, pitched into their troughs, then turned tail very carefully and crept back to Marine East. With three weeks of vacation we need not risk life and ship; besides, one has to be some kind of masochist to tolerate a day's suffering in angry seas.

Back at the dock, Joe washed the boat again. Afterward, we hiked, browsed marine supply stores, found a supermarket and stocked up on fresh food, and exchanged yarns with other voyagers. We discovered once again that it pays to spend a full day in each town.

The next morning, wind diminished, we set forth once again through Whitehead and Green Island Passages. Just looking at Casco Bay's lovely islands this time, we vowed on a future trip to linger. We passed Webster Rock, Lumbo Ledge and Cape Small; it was only 8:43 A.M. In two hours we had already seen what seemed to be hundreds of islands; it would take a year or more just to explore that small stretch of coast!

On our trip with Bobby we had taken an offshore route between Cape Small and Allen Island, which is one of perhaps fifty islands strewn across the wide mouth of the St. George River. On that course you see only ocean with the islands and headlands as specks in the distance. We studied our chart and chose an alternate route that would bring us close to those beckoning shores. At Cape Small we turned toward Jacknife Ledge inside Seguin Island, passed the rocks called "The Sisters" and the Sheepscot River Bell mid-way across Sheepscott Bay. With Damariscove Island to starboard we found the Cuckolds: a fifty-nine foot tower which can be seen for twenty-four miles. It stands just off the tip of Southport Island where it marks the entrance to fabled Boothbay Harbor.

Years before on an auto trip, Joe, Paul and I had boarded one of the Boothbay tour boats for a cruise to Squirrel Island where we spent several unforgettable hours. How we had yearned to be able to reach these lovely islands in our own boat. Here we were doing it!

We idled past spruce crowned Ocean Point on Linekin Neck with its old summer homes, hugged the steep shore of Thrumcap Island, then crossed Johns Bay to Pemaquid Ledge. It was still only 10:15 A.M.

We increased our speed to cross Muscongus Bay, seven miles of open water, to Eastern Egg Rock: twenty-three feet high and marked by a day beacon, it was still very hard to find in the confusion of buoys and dancing waves. Muscongus Bay is much frequented by small pleasure and fishing craft, but it can be nasty. Obstructed by numerous ledges and islands, foul ground and shoals, it is no place to be overtaken by fog.

We threaded our way through rocks, shoals and ledges, keeping the can on Old Hump Ledge ahead carefully aligned with Egg Rock Beacon astern, dangers all around. Engine throttled back to 1000 we crept through Davis Strait, past Marshall Point and The Brothers Islands, then rounded the bell at Mosquito Island (south of Tenants Harbor). It was just short of noon. What a morning. Unscathed we had come through a gorgeous, fearful maze.

We resumed using Bobby's courses through the Muscle Ridge Channel, but we could not yet resume speed. This channel, like so many in Maine, is thick with thousands of lobster traps, and their bobbing buoys lurk in unlikely places, ready to snare even the most cautious yachtsman. Lobster boats seldom get caught by them, no black magic protects them, they have cages around their propellers. If lobsters would remain in deep water as they do in winter, they would not constitute a problem, but, come spring, they congregate on reefs, shoals and ledges along the coast, exactly where the aids to navigation are most numerous. Smart lobstermen fish where the lobsters are!

We were advancing cautiously through Muscle Ridge Channel, dodging and weaving, trying to pick a clear path, eyes fixed on each buoy as it disappeared from sight beside our bow, cheering as it reappeared astern.

THUNK! Something heavy crashed into our bottom. Joe shifted into neutral and I ran to the stern. Sure enough, we had a tail! Rocks, shoals and ledges surrounded us. If the rope was tight around our propeller we would be immobilized, have to be towed in somewhere, hire a diver, or get the boat hauled: a dreadful prospect.

It could not be. Joe (thank God) is at his best in an emergency. Instructions snapped out:

"Get the boat hook. Now fish that buoy aboard. Pull all the rope in. Okay, give it a little slack while I reverse the engine. Now pull it again. Good. Slack off again. I'll reverse again, just a little ... pull ... it's in neutral ... pull ... "

I pulled the mangled tail of rope aboard. It was a fairly old line, but even a new one is no match for a big diesel engine. If the rope had not broken we would have been stuck. This time we were lucky, the lobsterman was not as his loss amounted to thirty or forty dollars for trap, line and buoy!

Joe kept listening to our engine, wondering if shaft or prop had been damaged, if any line remained around the prop, or if the trap had damaged the hull. Worry, worry. Silent and anxious we crept along the very narrow channel through breath-taking Owls Head Bay. Leaving the "C3" can to port we fled across turbulent Penobscot Bay toward Stand-In Point on North Haven Island.

The beautiful Fox Island Thorofare stretched before us: seven miles of shelter, easy to navigate on a clear day, numerous scenic coves offering good anchorage. We pondered the alternatives. We were only two hours from Bass Harbor, and it was just 2:30 P.M. Up to this point we had been in a hurry to get to Maine. Well, we were here, why not spend the night and explore this island?

Paul and Jeanne on a hill on North Haven Island.
LADY JEANNE, tied to yacht club dock. Opposite shore is Vinalhaven.

We eased in close to the yacht club float. Down the ramp strode the club captain, all smiling welcome. To our query about safe anchorages or available guest moorings he replied:

"Why, you can spend the night right here at the dock if you let me take a look at your boat. One of Bob Rich's if I'm not mistaken, I can tell her by her lines, She's a beauty!"

There is no better news! I scurried forward and tossed the bow line to that hospitable gentleman. He secured it expertly in a single motion, and went aft to take the stern line and hold us off while I lowered bumpers. Soon he was aboard being given a royal tour by the captain. There is scarcely anything more enjoyable than showing off your lovely boat to a knowledgeable, appreciative seaman, especially when you had helped design her. Our visitor turned out to be an old friend of Bobby's.

Tour over, Joe washed the boat, then we went ashore for a long hike. There are few cars on the island so hiking the roads is pleasant and the views are everywhere bewitching. We did some shopping in the small store.

We never bring everything we will need on a trip, since talking to shop-keepers is an invaluable way to gather local knowledge. They have a living to make and we take up their time with questions; we try to repay their courtesy at the check out counter.

The word had gone out that the fancy lobster boat at the yacht club had a bath tub (no kidding), and when we returned we found a few club members gathered admiringly on the dock. Another tour was offered and accepted. No one overstayed their welcome, and soon peace was restored and dinner in the making. We thought: *"now we are in Maine!"*

The next morning we made a leisurely start with a sparkling LADY JEANNE. We were going to bring her home in top condition, show Bobby how well we had cared for her. Slow across a calm West Penobscot Bay, through the Deer Isle Thorofare, across Jericho Bay, through the York Narrows north of Swans Island and, finally, the last course: 83° for six miles across Blue Hill Bay to Weaver Ledge in Bass Harbor. How we thrilled at the sight of the water towers, visible for miles out to sea. We had made it! We were home! Home!

Bob and Mildred were somewhat surprised to see us. Most folks sail away with their boats, never to return. Bobby teased Joe about not getting the boat wet. I guess he never knew anyone who kept a boat the way Joe does. He gets it wet; then he gets it clean again ... always and soon!

Joe was still worried about the possible damage from the lobster trap we'd picked up, and he also felt that the bottom could use another coat of paint, he decided to change the depth sounder. Bobby agreed to haul the boat the next day.

We didn't want to be underfoot while the boat was being worked on, so we planned a busy day. Right after breakfast we rowed across Bass Harbor to the ferry terminal, tied our dinghy to the town landing, and took the ferry to Swans Island, something we had long promised ourselves we would do. When we got off the ferry we started walking toward Burnt Coat Harbor, on the far side of the island. It was really hot in the middle of the island and what had looked like perhaps three miles on the map was more like five or six. After we'd climbed a couple of long hills, we really thought we'd made a mistake. What a scatter-brained plan! We were about to turn back when someone stopped and asked if we wanted a lift. We accepted thankfully and were soon enjoying the splendid view of Burnt Coat Harbor: lobster fleet, lighthouse and sheltering islands. We shopped for lunch makings at the country store (now Hindeman's Cash and Carry), climbed a blueberry hill overlooking the harbor, had a lovely picnic and then picked blueberries. In Maine I am always prepared for berry-picking!

Since there are no inns on the island, we had to make the last ferry; we started back in good time. Our brisk pace soon faltered in the heat. Just in time, a car stopped. A lovely oriental lady asked if we'd like a ride. She was a scientist from Woods Hole who was spending a few days as a guest on the island. She said everyone else was working in the garden but she was hiding. We all laughed. Since we had plenty of time to make the ferry, she offered to drive us around the island. We exchanged histories, then stopped to pick raspberries together. She was so happy and friendly. What a good experience. We have never walked too far on that island without being offered a ride. The local people never miss a chance to talk to a visitor. We have entertainment value for them; island life is limited in what it offers. I guess they get tired of talking to each other.

On the ferry ride back to Bass Harbor we marvelled again at the beautiful view of Mount Desert Island's mountains. It had been a wonderful day ... and it was not over yet. Walking up from the ferry terminal we saw a *for sale* sign on an ancient, tiny house across from the old fish factory and water towers. We walked up to Reed's store and called the owner. He wanted $6,000 for the house, and he was eager to sell. His mother had been living in the house, but it needed more renovating than anyone in the family could afford. If they sold it, they could buy a trailer for her and set it up on her son's land.

I don't know how anyone could have lived in that house: the roof leaked, there was no well or septic system, the outhouse and attached shed were falling down, the yard was overgrown and strewn with a hundred year's accumulation of junk, there was no basement and the foundation stones were loose and missing, the windows were rotten and the house was right next to the street. It would be endless hard work and quite a lot of money before it could be restored, but we had long hungered for a little place in Maine ... a start.

In spite of all the drawbacks there were some positive aspects: the price was right, we could not tie up much money, the house was small, only 16' x 20' so it would not take forever to fix and, even if we completely renovated it, that small a house can't absorb too much material. Best of all, there was a beautiful view of Bass Harbor from the second floor front window, and six gorgeous mountains could be seen from the back window. I envisioned a cozy studio apartment with deck on the second floor, a workshop and small boat storage space on the first floor, and a fruit and vegetable garden in the long back yard. A land base in Maine!

We offered young Bob $5,500, which he accepted. We gave him a small deposit; we would have to raise the money when we got back to New York. We were big Maine land-owners: a 16' x 20' house on a 35' x 120' lot!

By the time we got back to the LADY JEANNE Bobby had her back in the water, all work completed. The lobster trap had not caused any damage. Joe had worried needlessly.

During the following week we really experienced the fabulous harbors of Mount Desert Island. We poked down Somes Sound (a real fiord), its entrance graced by enormous estates, followed by a panorama of sheltering mountains: Flying, St. Sauveur, Valley Clifts and Acadia on the west, Norumbega to the east. Paul had a chance to run the boat since we could see where we were going and the dangers were well marked. On long offshore courses or in dangerous, unfamiliar waters we could not permit our twelve year old to take the helm, to his chagrin. We anchored in Valley Cove to swim in icy water, hike mountain trails and picnic on the beach. We picked up a mooring near Bar Island and watched the Osprey family in their giant nest, walked all around that jewel-like island, then rowed around visiting yachts and into hidden coves. We took the dinghy to the town landing where a short walk through picturesque Somesville led to Fernald's Store. They had everything we needed (as most general stores in Maine do), and seeing that we were struggling to apportion our bulky purchases, they insisted on taking us back to the boat.

The next day we called the dock master in Northeast Harbor and reserved a guest mooring in the crowded, world-famous harbor. From that secure base we explored the graceful community with its huge cedar shingled summer "cottages." This is still one of the most "in" places for rusticating. We rowed to the Asticou Wharf and climbed to Thuya (cedar) Lodge which contains the noted Curtis collection of botanical books, marvelled at the exquisite formal gardens, then went out the back gate to climb Eliot Mountain. The endless mountain trails which can be reached from this spot could keep one busy for weeks. The town is at the heart of Mount Desert Island which encompasses 108 square miles of which 30,000 acres belong to Acadia National Park, this is a paradise on earth featuring a spectacular range of granite mountains, seven summits of which exceed a thousand feet in elevation. There are a score of glacial lakes and ponds, a 55 mile network of carriage roads, and 120 miles of delightful woodland, shore and mountain trails.

We picked blueberries every day; they grow everywhere. Browsing the many shops, we found crafts unique to the area, as well as everything else one could desire. At the Pine Tree Market we again found a staff ready to fill every need and then deliver to the dock.

Later we found a town mooring in Southwest Harbor and from that base we cruised around the islands: Great and Little Cranberry, Baker, Placentia, Black, and Great and Little Gott. These have to be some of the world's most beautiful islands: pink granite headlands, sand or gravel beaches, deep quiet forests filled with deer and thousands of bright birds and flowers, quiet sun-drenched coves. Safe on a good mooring near town we enjoyed the evening bustle: yachts from all over anchoring for the night, the schooner fleet from Camden coming and going with all sails spread, the Coast Guard responding to calls from ships in distress, often someone who had picked up a lobster buoy.

All too soon it was August 6th, the day set for beginning our return voyage. How we would miss the cormorants drying their wings while they perched on piling, rock or navigation buoy; the porpoises which romped through the harbors, babies following their mothers; the harbor seals which basked in the sun at Bunkers Ledge or surfaced suddenly like smiling dogs or clutching a fish between their teeth.

We left Bass Harbor at mid-day, planning to make the four hour run to Tenants Harbor, a scheme which would result in two short days of cruising to Portland, rather than one long one.

Fog began to close in behind us and a wind sprang up, strong from the east, as we neared Tenants Harbor. We were thankful for this well protected harbor close to the route. Its lighted bell at the entrance and shores free of dangers make it a favorite lay-over for cruising folk. A service wharf on the north shore supplied fuel, water and fresh fish, as well as a guest mooring for the night. We were well prepared for anchoring but when cruising in unfamiliar waters the bottom is an unknown; when anchored, we dare not venture far from the boat; once moored, however, we could take long exploratory hikes without worry.

After a long ramble we were content to enjoy a leisurely dinner aboard. Our fresh fish was delicious. We tried to have Paul's favorite foods often and otherwise make the trip pleasant for him. Quite a gardener himself, he enjoyed the lovely gardens in these small villages. We took time to savor them.

The next morning was clear and calm; after a substantial breakfast in an inn overlooking the harbor, we cast off and made an uneventful passage over now familiar courses to South Portland where, once again, we stayed at Marine East. Portland is not a quiet place to sleep with the many tankers plying the Fore River, frequent flights overhead bound for the International Jetport, and heavy local traffic across the bridge, but it is an interesting city within reach of the route, and we felt at home there since this was our third visit by sea.

The next morning we woke to find our world had disappeared, blanketed in impenetrable cotton-wool fog. The mournful fog horn tolled throughout the day. We took to the streets again, crossing the draw bridge to Portland's Commercial Street, then turning right to the Old Port Exchange with its many shops and restaurants. Living aboard, we enjoyed the pleasures of city life without the expense of motels and restaurants (except for lunch). Someday we plan to stay a week, visit museum, civic center, and theater, and shop to our heart's content for just about anything.

The next morning in anticipation of the twelve hour day ahead we were up at dawn. Paul picked up his sleeping bag, and leaving his cot for us to stow, scurried below where he buried himself for several more hours of shut-eye. The sky was a sparkling blue with drifting cotton-candy clouds, the wind was moderate, and our route would be over tested off-shore courses.

Our day assumed its usual cruising rhythm: I plotted our courses on the first chart and then made breakfast, which we took turns eating in the wheelhouse. Breakfast over, I took the helm for a two hour watch, steering and keeping the log while Joe did the dishes and got the boat ship-shape. Joe loves a sparkling boat and he's willing to do the work of keeping it that way, one of the reasons cruising has always been so pleasant for me. While Joe took his two hours at the wheel I would lay out the next courses, keep the log, and prepare the meals. While traveling there was no time for loafing, both of us were busy. Cruising the coast is not the same as harbor-hoping in familiar waters. Whoever is steering must keep eyes glued to compass and horizon on the lookout for the next bell or whistle, as well as watch the water dead ahead for logs, lobster buoys or other dangers.

In coastal cruising serious navigation becomes a necessity. I have known hundreds of people who have had boats all their lives and never owned or used a real chart: one prepared by the U. S. Coast and Geodetic Survey. Having grown up on the water, fishing or harbor hopping with family and friends, they have "local knowledge" which serves their needs; they never venture out of familiar areas. Many Maine fishermen use no charts; they started fishing with their fathers as youngsters and they know the fishing grounds: every reef, shoal and deep. They don't use their work boats for pleasure, never leave home country.

Equipped with radar, loran and an automatic pilot, navigation is pretty foolproof. Without these aids, one must use a system known as dead-reckoning, (if you goof up I reckon you're dead). The accuracy of this system is estimated as plus or minus ten percent of distance travelled since the last fix. On a thirty mile leg there is a good chance that you will be three miles away from your goal at the estimated time of arrival. On a clear day with over five miles of visibility and a calm sea you will spot your buoy easily. Let the visibility drop to two miles and the seas increase, chances are good that you won't find your buoy. Those of us who use D R to navigate should stay in port when visibility is poor or when heavy weather is forecast. Like it or not, we're fair weather boaters.

Successful piloting also requires advance preparation: all necessary charts, drafting instruments and publications at hand, charts in the order of use: (detailed chart of the harbor you are leaving, beneath that the harbor approach chart, then the coastal chart, reversing that order for your destination). It gets to be quite a pile.

The most important information for any D R position is an accurate knowledge of the course and speed made good over ground. A reliable engine and a sea-worthy boat make all the difference here; in a good boat you can maintain speed with safety. I was especially pleased that our Rich boat made exactly 12 knots at 1850 rpm because the boat was usually comfortable at that speed, the engine perked smoothly, and my arithmetic was easy. I would measure the distance from one buoy to the next. If it was six miles, I knew that as long as we steered carefully we would reach the buoy in thirty minutes, and we did! Most of the time you can measure your course, maintain your speed and arrive on schedule, but sea-going adventures are not made of that sissy stuff; in real life, the wind picks up and you have to reduce speed, fog or rain reduce or eliminate visibility, or the helmsman dozes and wanders off course.

I tried to keep checking the accuracy of our headings by comparing the readings on the depth sounder with the depths on the chart. I also took the bearings of land marks like water towers, church steeples and light houses with a hand-bearing compass. The object is to stay on the line you have drawn from buoy to buoy, and to know at every ten minute interval exactly where you are on that line. Then, if you have to reduce throttle, you can re-compute your estimated time of arrival (ETA). By making these frequent checks you can avoid the panic that accompanies a no-show: time up and no buoy!

When you can't find the buoy you have to set up a careful search pattern, usually a square if there are no dangers nearby, until you find it. Prevention is better; lost buoys are frightening.

In addition to the charts and publications already mentioned, we always carry a marine atlas, waterway guide and cruising guide for the New England Coastal area. These give much additional information about available services which you hope you'll never require.

From Portland, through the Cape Cod Canal to Onset, is a long day at sea. We pulled into the Onset Marina at 6:00 P.M., tired and relieved; most of the long passages were behind us. One more day and we would be home.

The next morning it was almost 7:30 A.M. when we cast off. While it was clear and calm in Onset, Buzzards Bay was its usual gusty self. Instead of heading right down the middle as we had planned, we returned as we had come, back by Old Cock, determined to master that nasty section of coast. We didn't get disoriented this time and we felt better for facing our fear. We cleared Elisha Ledge, the R "2" Bell at Sakonnet Point and Point Judith, but after that I did not make another entry in the log, except to show a reduction of speed to 1200 rpm. I just hung on. Paul and Joe, ditto! From Point Judith to Dering Harbor is about fifty miles of Block Island Sound ... and it was nasty. I hate to say this, but it is often nasty. We didn't cook, we didn't take pictures. I didn't get any fixes on the lighthouses and towers. We all simply endured. Once in a while someone would say:

"I wish we'd gone into the harbor of refuge at Point Judith." Or:

"Maybe we should have gone behind Fishers Island and spent the night at Mystic."

Helpful suggestions, but all too late. We were committed, and we pushed on. When we picked up our mooring in Dering Harbor at 4:30 P.M., we were all worn out. Offshore cruising is demanding, exciting and challenging, but seldom restful.

During this trip to Maine with Paul along Joe had tried valiantly to enjoy his dream come true, tried especially to make it a memorable experience for Paul, since this might be his last extended cruise with us. We realized that once children reach adolescence they have less interest in family outings.

Despite his best efforts, it was often apparent that all was not right with Joe. He over-reacted to every problem; always before, he had been quick with a cheerful solution for every situation. He became more dependent, afraid to let me out of his sight, sure that something would happen to me. He found fault with everything. I was reading everything possible about depression, looking for insights. He refused to read about it, saying it only made him feel worse. His hands and face seemed to be puffy and he often said he felt worried ... "just worried."

Late in August we took Elaine and a college friend for an outing on the boat but it was not a great success, Joe was too nervous. Soon after, Joe insisted on bringing LADY JEANNE to the marina in Coecles Harbor for still more painting, this time of cabin decks and sides. It seemed irrational to me since we'd be hauling in a couple of months, but Joe would not listen to reason.

On Friday, September 2 Joe woke up at 5:00 A.M. crying bitterly. He begged:

"Help me. Take me somewhere! I can't stay here like this."

I called our family doctor and he gave Joe an appointment for 4:45 P.M. That was to be the longest day of my life. Joe cried and begged me to help him. He wouldn't eat, dress, shave, read, or listen to the radio. There was nothing he could do but cry and toss. I had no idea what to do except try to calm him until we could get to the doctor.

The doctor gave Joe a needle, some kind of tranquilizer, but told him that since his illness was mental it was beyond his own area of expertise. He had already given Joe a very thorough physical and found no problem there. He said we had three choices: he could recommend a private psychiatrist or a private mental hospital, or Joe could sign himself in at the state mental hospital at Central Islip. He gave Joe some capsules which he hoped would get him through the weekend while we decided what to do, but there was NO way we could get through that weekend. We were supposed to take Elaine back to Wellesley College on Sunday and then go on to Maine to pay for our little house. Jeanne and Chris agreed to take Elaine; the house would have to wait.

After a restless night Joe woke up and starting crying again, saying he could not stand "it" another day, insisting that I must take him to the hospital. The capsules had only dulled the pain slightly; his anguish was terrible to see.

I called my brother, John, who is a psychiatrist, and asked his advice. He told me to take Joe to Central Islip where he would be helped. He assured me that the doctors there would know what to do for him, and since John had worked in that hospital for ten years I thought he should know what was best.

At noon Chris drove Joe and me to the hospital which is a big brick, rather carelessly maintained complex. Rock and roll music blared in the waiting room, the receptionist seemed unprofessional: poorly groomed and constantly smoking, upstairs a man was out ôf control, banging and banging on a door. We waited for two hours in that din before a woman doctor took us into her office to hear our tale of anxiety and depression that no amount of escape could alleviate. We had been running from this illness for two years ... now it was upon us.

Joe signed himself in, but with understandable reluctance, as what he had seen of the hospital had not increased his confidence. We were both crying when I tore myself away. Joe looked like a lost, frightened child. I hated to leave him, but I did not know what else to do. I had walked a thousand miles, offered a thousand encouragements. I did not know how to help Joe. Chris and I drove home in silence. That evening the children gathered, offering comfort and hope, but there is not much comfort when mental illness strikes. It is a lonely scourge. We had tried so hard, worked so much. Why? Why?

The doctors tried Joe on the usual medicines for depression, but they all had unacceptable side effects. After a few days they prescribed electric shock therapy. I had read about this and knew it to be controversial, but drugs were not working and Joe was in such pain. We agreed to try it.

After two treatments with ECT Joe felt markedly better. The doctors agreed that he could come home; they would give him further treatments when needed as an out-patient. We cut our work week to just three days, spending the other four days on the LADY JEANNE in Dering Harbor, then in Coecles Harbor where we planned to haul for the winter. That last ride around Shelter Island was more sorrowful than I can say; we wondered if we would ever again enjoy a cruise in our lovely boat.

On September 24th we turned our children's day nursery into a festive hall to celebrate Marie's wedding to Peter Spindler. This happy event brought a fine carpenter into the family and left us with only three unmarried children, but Joe looked like a ghost as he walked down the aisle with our sweet little daughter.

On November 2nd, Joe had his eighth shock treatment. After each treatment he would have a few days of blessed relief, then deteriorate again into weeping and inability to function. Each time we would hope that the improvement would last. On two occasions he got up in the night and turned on the gas, then woke me, weeping, to say he didn't even have the courage to kill himelf. By December 7th, Joe'd had fifteen shock treatments and was more in control of himself. The doctors urged him to try another drug, Nardil, one of the MAO inhibitors, which had been found very useful in the treatment of depressed workaholics. Joe would have to observe some dietary restrictions: no cheese, chocolate, coffee or alcohol. Only the coffee was hard. It took some weeks but at last Joe began to be able to work and sleep. It seemed like a miracle. Hope stirred.

By mid-December Joe was so encouraged that we decided if he continued to improve we would take a winter vacation to the south. The day after our family Christmas Joe, Paul and I began a three week auto trip, stopping first in Pittsburgh to spend a couple of days with Michele and her family.

1978

On January 1st our daughter Jeanne gave birth to her first child and our third grandchild, winsome Beth. When that news reached us, we were in Tennessee trying unsuccessfully to visit the Smokey Mountain National Park. Only cars with chains were allowed into the snow covered park; and we who had none were refused admittance. The next day we stopped in Plains, Georgia, President Carter's home town. Then we drove on to Florida and the Keys for ten days of sun at the Tropic Aire Resort in Lower Matecumbe. We stayed in a very clean and beautiful efficiency apartment and there was a lovely beach right on the grounds. Paul's current hobby was tropical fish and he was in heaven, finding and identifying. We all enjoyed the many beautiful and strange birds, especially the pelicans which fed near our beach. We picked limes, lemons and oranges and soaked up the sun. On the way north we visited Disney World, staying in a camper trailer right on the grounds, and Silver Springs, which turned out to be a very worthwhile tourist attraction. The only Florida vacation of our lives was a success: Joe held up, kept busy with all the driving. Except for one repair ($93) the car held up. I stepped on a nail and needed an emergency room stop for a tetanus shot ($38).

It was fortunate that we had a good rest as only days after our return the blizzard of '78 dumped eighteen inches of snow! To the shovels EVERYONE! A week later a sudden thaw brought floods. Joey's house was inundated; Joey, Nancy and Jason moved in with us while Joey moved his oil burner upstairs and cleaned up; then, only days later, their second son, Ian, was born.

After the floods receeded we drove to Shelter Island to check on the boat. Because of the shock treatments, Joe had lost much of his recent memory; he couldn't remember what the boat looked like or even where it was. (Most of this memory loss was recovered in time.) The boatyard crew was almost finished painting LADY JEANNE and she looked wonderful.

Joe's memory gradually returned, and the drug kept him functioning, but he was far from really well. He became more and more compulsive, often working until midnight and then sleeping poorly. I didn't get much sleep either. His personality changed, at times he just had to buy something, whether we needed it or not. A few times when he felt anxious he did the worst possible thing: bought a bottle of whiskey and polished it off. This was something he had never done before.

Late in March Michele and Peter arrived for a week's visit with us and the three cousins. Soon after, we hired Marie's husband Peter to renovate the porch on the nursery. We made arrangements with a Maine carpenter to put a new roof on our little Maine house and made a quick trip to Maine to record the deed. The nursery was filled to capacity. Another busy year. Joe was staying up later and later, never satisfied with the day's work. We were certainly going to need our Maine vacation. Elaine was home from college; she would manage the nursery and keep Paul out of mischief, and we were off!

COECLES HARBOR TO BASS HARBOR and RETURN July 1978

On the first of July we went aboard for a six week vacation. Before leaving, Joe had several new purchases to install. We were ready on the fifth but wind, rain and high seas made us wait a day.

At 5:15 A.M. on July 6th we left Coecles Harbor; we planned to return on August 14th, our twins' eighteenth birthday. Our first day took us over familiar courses to the Cape Cod Canal, but a mean following sea in Buzzards Bay kept us on our toes. Not surprisingly, the next day was too rough; we laid over in Onset where we took a long walk, shopped and rowed around Wicketts Island.

The next day promised beautiful cruising: wind at twelve knots from the southwest, we would be in the lee, sky clear, temperature at 69°F. We made good time through Cape Cod Bay, 8.5 n.m. to R "12" but we found the buoy well to our port. The next course was worse: we were fifteen minutes late reaching the BW "H" whistle. Too much for a seventy-five minute leg. Were the tide, wind and current responsible or were we steering less carefully? Our winter ashore had not improved our skills. We found the R "2" whistle at Cape Ann on schedule and began the twenty-six mile run to York Ledge Whistle. Twenty minutes after we were supposed to find that buoy we sighted the Murray Rock can, two miles to the west; since we came up to it from the southwest we must have been four miles off course. Panic ensued while I studied the chart. The buoy marked a big shoal. Waves hissing, and the next buoy out of sight, though only two miles distant, I plotted a new course. We must have been edging toward land to be so far off; we have made that dangerous error several times in deteriorating weather. On days like this radar seems like a very desirable option.

Fog and rain closed in behind us when we reached Portland; it would be three days before we could stir. We took our ease in port, savoring the good life, trying to break the hurry habit. No more long days. We would explore Casco Bay.

On Tuesday afternoon a short hop through Green Island Passage, across Broad Sound and up Merriconeag Sound led to Mackerel Cove on Bailey Island where we found a berth at the Brookside Marina. Excitement was high in anticipation of the annual Tuna Tournament. We were tempted to stay, but all the berths were already reserved. We explored, shopped and swapped yarns with our neighbors.

The next day we idled up Quahog Bay, past Pole Island to Orrs Cove on Sebascodegan Island, a beautiful area with hundreds of storybook homes clinging to rocks and hidden in tiny coves. The marina had a guest mooring which we enjoyed for a couple of days. Bikini clad, we scandalized the natives while working on our tans, then dressed and went ashore to explore that paradise, and watch the restoration of an antique Herreshoff sloop.

We scurried over to Sebasco harbor early on Friday morning. We had been advised that there were guest moorings at this favorite resort but that by noon Friday they would all be occupied. By 9:00 A.M. we were secured to a mooring, and the club launch was circling to inform us of available services and offer us a lift ashore. What luxury! This beautiful complex has everything: restaurant, golf course, movies, snack bar and launch service. It developed that they also had plenty of fog that year.

One evening we went for a long walk and arrived back at the harbor to find it completely socked in; we couldn't see our boat or any familiar boat. The harbor isn't too big, so we set out to find LADY JEANNE; we headed in what we thought was the right direction, rowed and rowed, only to find ourselves all the way into the head of the harbor where remembered ledges near Harbor Island blocked our way. I don't know how we would have found our boat if there had not been a local fisherman tending his own boat nearby. He remembered seeing our L J in the harbor and started us in the right direction, correcting our heading until we were out of his sight and giving us descriptions of the next boats en route. We were shook up when we reached safety; imagination has such power: we had pictured ourselves wandering out of the harbor and being lost at sea. We decided that a pocket compass should be part of our shore-going gear. We don't automatically orient ourselves to directions as old salts do, and dense fog can confuse almost anyone.

The next day in somewhat improved visibility we rowed past Burnt Coat Island to West Point and climbed a long ladder from a fish dock to an authentic country store: pot-bellied stove, spittoon and much more. We bought our lunch and then explored that little town.

Sunday afternoon a fresh breeze took out the fog and we cast off; after two and a half days we were ready for a change. The breeze was too spirited, however. We got as far as Wood Island Bell to find Casco Bay sporting mountainous seas. We scooted back to our Sebasco mooring; between fog and wind it seemed we'd never get around Cape Small. We went ashore on Harbor Island where I gave Joe a haircut.

It was 1:30 P.M. on Monday before the wind subsided enough for us to escape: around Cape Small, across Sheepscot, Booth, Johns and Muscongus Bays, through the Georges Islands and outside Mosquito Island to the now familiar shelter of Tenants Harbor. How pleasant it was making short hops from one beautiful harbor to another on this breath-taking Maine coast.

The next day we crossed Penobscot Bay through the Fox Islands Thorofare, then passed through the Deer Island Thorofare intent on finding a secure anchorage on Deer Isle. We had visited that island by car many times and had marvelled at the beauty of its coves, each one a jewel. We wanted to tuck ourselves into such a cove and absorb some of that serene majesty; we imagined a hideaway off the route where we could sunbathe and explore.

We found just the place in Southeast Harbor, protected by Whitmore Neck, with good secure anchorage in fifteen feet of water, idyllic coves, safe from any storm. Only one vessel, a classy sailing yacht, was anchored in the entire area, and they were well away from us. Peace.

We savored that retreat until our food ran low and, by then, we were ready for the world again. Hoisting anchor, we confirmed the makeup of the bottom: nice black mud. Joe climbed into the dinghy and thoroughly washed the anchor before hauling it aboard. It really is difficult to get anchors clean enough to bring aboard a spotless boat; one reason we use moorings whenever they are available.

Back to the route and through York Narrows, then across Blue Hill Bay ... there they are ... the water towers of Bass Harbor! Right behind the towers is our tiny Maine house, waiting for us!

Bobby Rich made room for us in his little marina. Plugged in, we could operate without running the generator, a plus. We talked to Bobby about our ideas for another boat. Designing boats is such fun, and we were beginning to feel that we'd like some changes: no generator and an enclosed wheelhouse, for starters, but he seemed tired. He slept so poorly. His health was failing and his old spirit was sadly diminished; he said he doubted that he'd live long enough to build another boat. How sad we were to find him so low. We put new boat thoughts aside for the time. We were eager to get to our house.

Over the winter we had hired a local contractor to tear down and haul away the shed and outhouse and a carpenter to shingle the roof. Since the roof boards were completely rotten, they had to be replaced. The new roof cost $2,500! That was much more than we had anticipated and we hoped he had done a good job.

We rowed across the harbor and hauled our dinghy up the long stony beach by Maurice Rich's lobster pier, tied it to an old dock and crossed the road to our Ferry Road house. We were armed for battle with hammers, crow bars and scrapers we had carried from New York in anticipation of this challenge, well-stocked picnic cooler, Coleman stove, portable radio and coffee pot.

The new roof looked good. The house was ready for the next fifty years. It stood erect, at least. We would make a beginning this summer. Besides, all the sitting, resting and good eating were having their usual effects: pounds and inches. We needed some work. And, work it was!

Our goal for this year was to completely gut the house. All old beaver board, cheap panelling, wet sheetrock, soggy insulation, flimsy partitions, etc. would go out. But, first, I washed the old windows until they shone. Every time we looked up from our work, we could feast our eyes on the dancing water of Bass Harbor and Blue Hill Bay or the friendly mountains of Mount Desert. True, the water was seen between the legs of the water towers, but its blueness was undiminished.

We began upstairs, prying, pulling and pitching with fierce enthusiasm. There is something about demolition which sets adrenalin pumping. A couple of days at that fever pitch and we could sweep and set up a camp on the second floor. On our June trip to Maine by car we had brought a couple of foam mattresses, blankets and sleeping bags, a card table, lawn chairs, gardening tools and curtains.

Each evening we rowed back to LADY JEANNE, took a bath, enjoyed our supper and slept, but during daylight hours we worked on the house, and once our little camp was established we enjoyed our lunches up there with our view.

Joe had a great idea. Since we could sleep in the house, at least for a couple of days, why not get the boat's topsides painted here in Maine. We knew Jim Rich would do a good job, and we never liked to put paint on in the winter, when it was too hard to find a warm enough day. Jim said he could fit us in, so we brought the boat to Duck Cove to be hauled and we hitched a ride back to our camp.

Unfortunately, the weather failed to cooperate. It rained. Then the fog settled in. A job that should have taken two days stretched into ten. Our camp had no bathroom, so our resourcefulness was tested as never before. We could get water from our next door neighbors, but we wouldn't bother them too often. We took turns using available bathrooms in marinas, ferry terminal, stores and the homes of friends; we set up a grooming area with wash basin and shaving mirror and bought a chamber pot for emergencies and night time use. We had kerosene lanterns and basic housekeeping equipment, everything we really needed, so it turned into an adventure we will always remember. We learned so much about surviving in that ten days. We kept clean and well nourished. Truly, we had our own Outward Bound experience.

Once the lower floor was gutted we had a bonfire to get rid of all the burnable rubbish, then we hired Dick Hamblen to grade the property and bring gravel for a driveway on the side and a patio behind the house. In Maine if you don't get some gravel down, you will always be stuck in the mud. That done, we raked and graded, piled stones along the drive and patio, cut the dead trees along the brook at the rear property line. The soil was good, grass and wildflowers sprang up as soon as we finished. By next year we would need a lawnmower.

We called the electric company and had the power connected, hung curtains on the old windows, connected a light to a timer, and installed new locks. The house was bare and empty except for our upstairs camp, but we didn't want to encourage vandalism. We hoped it would appear occupied when we left.

Once the boat was back in the water, sparkling for another year, we cruised around Baker Island again, and watched the seals at Bunker Ledge, then went down Somes Sound to spend a night on a mooring at Hall Quarry where we picked blueberries. We also checked the osprey nest at Bar Island and visited Fernald's Store in Somesville. Everywhere we went folks remembered us from our previous visits and we began to feel more and more at home. The thought of returning to New York became ever harder to bear. We went back to Bass Harbor to say our farewells to Mildred and Bobby, and on August 10th we started our return journey.

It was 12:30 P.M. before we got off, but we had a short haul planned: only to Camden by way of Eggemoggin Reach, a new route for us. Instead of using York Narrows we crossed Blue Hill Bay to the Ships and Barges Ledge then took Pond Island Passage to Eggemoggin Reach. There, we checked out the harbors we had visited by car: Center Harbor where Joel White's Brooklin Boat Yard is located, and the Benjamin River Boatyard. For the very first time we steamed under the high Deer Isle Bridge. How many times had we crossed that bridge, looking longingly at the brilliant water below. Then our route led us past Cape Rosier, where we saluted Scott and Helen Nearing, esteemed ecologists, whose stone house overlooks that passage.

We continued down East Penobscot Bay to Islesboro where we poked into renowned Dark Harbor, then nervously proceeded across Jobs Island Bar. Bobby had given us very specific instructions about how to safely cross this "local knowledge only" shortcut; our cruising guide advised a rising tide and slow motion. We observed all cautions, lined the buoys exactly, and made a safe crossing. In half an hour we were tying up at Camden's town dock. We were lucky to get that berth and other travelers should not depend on it; the dock master was just going off duty and since we planned to leave before 7:00 A.M. he allowed us to spend the night there. We were supposed to take on fuel in Camden at a pier operated by a friend of Bobby's, but his docks were already overcrowded. We decided to put off fueling till the morning.

Boat lovers gathered on the dock, admired the LADY JEANNE and we basked in that appreciation. Finally, we tore ourselves away and fixed supper, so it was after nine when we started out for an evening walk around town.

We didn't get too far. As we strolled past the Bay Street Garage the unmistakable strains of "Take Five" reached us. We had no plan to party, but the lure was irresistible. We went into that cozy nightclub to find a talented band belting out the music of our lifetime. The dance floor was small but adequate, the libations potent. We ended up dancing until two in the morning, enjoying the music with a platter of cheese and fruit and more manhattans than we ever had. Relieved that we had no car to worry about, clinging to each other, we cautiously returned to the waterfront, boarded LADY JEANNE, and crawled into bunks that would not stay still. A restless night ensued, but we agreed that it was worth it. We'd had a wonderful, carefree evening, reminiscent of courting days.

In the morning all the fuel docks were still crowded; since we had to leave by 7:00 A.M. we decided to put off refueling until we got into Portland. It was one of those rare summer days, hardly a cloud and the water barely stirring. We rounded Mosquito Island at 9:00 A.M. and shot out into the Gulf of Maine to run the offshore course: past Allen Island, Bantam Rock off Boothbay, Mile Ledge off Seguin. It was only 11:30, we were making wonderful time, the water was glassy. At this rate we'd be in Portland by 1:30. How could we call an early halt on such a day? We would skip Portland and make time. I took the chart and drew a new course: 20 miles offshore from Seguin's Mile Ledge to the East Hue and Cry off Cape Elizabeth. What a day! It was just after one when we passed Cape Elizabeth. On to Cape Porpoise. Still only three! Why stop? Besides, Cape Porpoise has such a tiny harbor. Onward. We were invincible!

It was 7:00 P.M. when we rounded the whistle at Cape Ann. The sky was aflame with one of the most priceless sunsets in memory. We felt wonderful. We had made so many miles over such still water, and this the ocean. We were high with our sense of achievement.

Almost simultaneously, 'miles traveled' made us remember fuel. FUEL! We were supposed to refuel in Portland. My God! Joe reduced throttle then gave me the wheel while he raced for the fuel dipstick, muttering: "stupid ... stupid .." and worse. The stick showed just over three inches of fuel; we had no idea how much that was, the base of the tank was tapered, so it was not much. The fuel line came off the bottom; we had wanted it to come in from the top to avoid sediment in the fuel lines, but that detail had been overlooked when the tank was ordered. That might be to our advantage now.

I checked the chart and measured the distance to the Gloucester Harbor Whistle: 7.4 nautical miles, perhaps a few more, to a safe berth. I pulled out the cruising guide: the Eastern Point Yacht Club was right behind the breakwater at the harbor entrance, but it had no fuel. No matter. It was nearest. It was almost dark; we would try to make it to the Yacht club, secure the boat and find fuel in the morning.

We had no harbor chart for Gloucester, but the marine atlas did have a blow-up which seemed adequate, and the cruising guide described a shoal near the dock and the way to avoid it. Moving at half throttle to conserve fuel we crept into the harbor, hearts pounding, ears alert to catch the first gasp from the engine. The thought of dropping anchor in the dark, in the middle of that enormously busy, wide-open harbor entrance gave us the shivers. How could we have forgotten fuel? We had always refueled after every run. With a 170 gallon tank we should never run out of fuel while cruising the coast. We'd planned to see a friend of Bobby's in Camden and

John McCarty in Portland, either of whom would have cashed a check for us. We didn't even have enough cash to make it home. Would another marina accept a check or credit card? We only had $98 left! It was Friday. Banks are all closed on Saturday. Worse and worse.

"There's the breakwater ... drat! All the moorings seemed to be occupied, we'll have to chance the dock."

Joe nosed into the float and I jumped off with the bow line and secured. We could see that this was a pretty fancy club and the dock master was not cordial. We asked if there was a mooring we could use since he did not want us to tie up at the dock. None available. We explained our problem, insisting that we could go no further in the dark; we must spend the night there! He was unhappy, but he let us stay. We tied the LADY JEANNE as far in as possible to leave room for others on the float (no one used the room we left) and measured our fuel. Less than two inches remained.

As we relaxed with coffee after supper, a large party of elegantly dressed club members descended to board an excursion boat for a moonlight cruise down the Annisquam River. One of the dinner jacketed men came over to ask what make of boat ours was. Joe told him it was custom built in Maine to our specifications. We have never forgotten his air of genuine puzzlement; he could not understand the concept or, perhaps he had already had too many martinis. It was funny. Late that night we heard the party return, stumbling up the gang plank.

The next morning we inquired about getting fuel in a can, but as there was no place within walking distance we'd have to chance running the boat into the inner harbor. We would keep to one side of the channel; if we ran out of fuel we would anchor and later row in with a can. We idled past Tenpound Island and rounded Rocky Neck, where we found a marina in Smith Cove. The proprietor was not interested in taking a credit card, but told us where to find a bank which was open on Saturday mornings. We would use the last of our money for fuel. "Fill-er up," we said, "but stop at $98." The pump registered $93.30 for 170 gallons. We must have come in on fumes!

We crossed the channel to Harbor Cove where all kinds of fishing craft were berthed. Restaurants and shops crowded the waterfront, and seagulls wheeled in the bright sky. Fortunately, many fishing boats were out so we found an empty berth, tied the boat carefully, and hurried ashore where an obliging bank solved the cash problem. We could relax.

Leisurely we set about surveying the town, browsed through the shops, made a few purchases and sauntered back to the docks. We were extremely thankful to have come untouched through a misadventure which could have cost us our boat, our lives, or both, had the weather turned on us, but our joy was tempered by resolve never to get ourselves in THAT fix again! Happily enjoying ice cream cones, hand in hand we started down the pier to the waiting LADY JEANNE.

The gulls which had been frolicking so gaily in the morning sky were no longer aimless! They had found a target. While we were gone, a dragger, decks piled with fish, had pulled into the berth next to us. The gulls were mounting their assault on that booty from OUR boat! Hundreds, and I mean hundreds, of red-eyed monsters were swooping, darting and screaming, dripping blood, gore and guano, fighting each other for every bite. Our beautiful, once spotless, boat was a battlefield!

Joe threw the remains of his ice cream into the water and ran, swearing mightily and waving his arms futilely, down the gang plank with me at his heels, trying to finish my cone.

We leapt aboard and Joe grabbed a mop to wave at the terrorists, but they completely ignored him, so intent were they on getting every possible mouthful. It was useless. Leaving his shoes in the fouled cockpit, Joe went in and started the engine while I unfastened docklines. He backed impatiently into the channel, then called me to take the helm. When he pulled in the fenders he got a good look at the hull. It was streaked with oil, grease and fish guts. He could not decide where to put the fenders as they were dripping with greasy muck. Even the canvas curtains on the wheelhouse were streaked with droppings.

It was just twelve-thirty. It took an hour to run the eight miles to Newcomb Ledge Whistle and another hour for the next eight miles to Boston's lighted horn buoy. I dared not go any faster since Joe was climbing all over the boat, bitterly complaining as he furiously scrubbed and scoured. I plotted each course without comment and tried not to hear him.

The next objective was Whistle "21" off Cohasset Harbor; I ended up near Minots Ledge in mountainous seas. Samuel de Champlain almost came to grief on these same rocks four hundred years before, and I was sure we were goners. Joe was still scrubbing and I couldn't read the buoys in the waves and spume. I did what seemed best: turned sharply away from the coast. Once in deeper water the waves diminished and I found the whistle.

The next heading was 166°, 12 nautical miles to Farnham Rock, which I left to starboard at four-fifteen. I had not left the wheel, we had not eaten, and the seas were still steep. I guess I was punchy by then. I was supposed to be running a 173° course for the Manomet Point Whistle, but I was obviously trying to self-destruct. I saw a buoy where no buoy should be and checked the chart to find I was inside the N "10" which marked High Pine Ledge, a reef-awash at low water! Another narrow escape.

To put a finishing touch on that day a Coast Guard Cutter raced across our bow, scaring us witless. Blue light flashing, he obviously wanted us to stop. Our windows were dripping with spray and I had not noticed his approach. Intent on reaching Onset before dark I had been running at 1700 rpm, making about eleven knots. The officer said he had tried to reach us by radio telephone since we were exceeding the speed limit for the entrance to the canal. He advised reduced throttle and radio ON! I had forgotten: while transiting the canal all vessels must monitor Channel 16.

The remainder of that day has gone from my memory, which is probably just as well. My log says that we reached Onset at 7:30 P.M.

The next morning we wakened to an invisible world, famous New England fog. We spent a long Sunday resting impatiently in Onset, both rather unstrung from the rigors of that journey and anxious about getting home for the twins' birthday. Only one day more and we would be celebrating with Jeanne and Elaine. It was difficult to realize that they would be eighteen. How the years had flown.

It was clear in Onset when we wakened early the next morning, but the weatherman predicted fog. I chose to believe that he was unduly pessimistic (after all, this WAS a special day). I will never learn. I even took a picture of the sunrise that morning.

We left Onset at eight-thirty and were making good time right past the BW "BB" Buzzards Bay Bell when the fog closed in all around us. Joe wanted to turn back, but I convinced him that it was more risky to try to negotiate the channel with its countless dangers than in the open water. We would have to steer with resolute accuracy (something we had NOT been doing) to keep on our course. We slowed to 1500 rpm and watched the compass nervously, counting the minutes.

Soon Gong "8" appeared before us in the mist. One down! Then R "6". Amazingly, R "4" also materialized. We had never steered so accurately. Each buoy came out of the fog only a hundred feet ahead of us. We could have run them down. We started to gain a bit of confidence, but it was premature.

We made the "1" Whistle, then plunged into increasing seas to make the twelve mile run to "CC" off Newport Neck. Privately maintained, that buoy must have been too small to find in the fog. We reduced throttle still more and kept to our heading, ears alert for other boats or buoys. Fifteen minutes after we should have sighted the Newport Buoy we saw a glow ahead: the Breton Reef Light! That is an 87' tower with a very bright light and a horn which we should have been heading for in the first place. At that point we were really frightened. How we wished we had radar.

We took a new heading from Breton Reef to Point Judith, then on to the Watch Hill Whistle and Constellation Rock, all of which we found on schedule. We were still enfolded in fog, and could see no more than a few hundred feet, at best. As we cleared the bell at Gardiners Point the water tank on Plum Island suddenly appeared, floating magically in the billowing mist. The fog was lifting at last.

It was six-thirty when we docked at Coecles Harbor Marina. We were so drained we would have given anything for a good stiff drink, but our ship was dry. Fearing that Joe would be tempted to over-indulge when he felt depressed, I had refused to buy any alcohol, but now I was ready to make an exception. We hurried ashore, but the liquor stores closed just before we reached each one, and by the time we got to Riverhead the birthday party had disbanded; our family had concluded that we would not make it that day. We went alone to a local bar and broke the rules. We had a couple of good drinks with a big pizza.

As we talked over our coastal cruises Joe and I agreed that we especially enjoyed exploring Maine's dramatic bays. We loved the rock-strewn coast and spruce crowned islands set against the pure sky and lapped by crystal waters. We liked the people, friendly and down-to-earth. We would be happy if we could stay in Maine year round, then we wouldn't have to make the long offshore trip to get there. Those trips were a challenge and exciting, but dangerous. Joe still wanted to make them, but perhaps they were really too much for him.

Talk of moving to Maine became a question of 'when' rather than 'if.' During this year while Joe had gone through such a severe depression we had necessarily left our day nursery in other hands time after time. It had survived, but we realized that it would be better if we could find a good full-time manager. We had worked too hard. Perhaps it would be wise to take the pressure off, let Joe have time to get completely well.

In early September Michele gave birth to her second child, sweet Marie. Elaine went back to college and Paul entered high school. Soon after, Renee became engaged and Jeanne announced that she would produce our sixth grandchild. We plunged into a whirl of work at the nursery; September and October were always the busiest months. We were already homesick for Maine, so we decided that as soon as all the new children had made an adjustment to life in the nursery we would see if our head teacher, Marie Burding, would like to manage the nursery. If she agreed, we would take a fall cruise, store the boat in Maine and, if all went well, follow our hearts and move permanently, taking Paul with us.

Because of our work load we were unable to get out to Shelter Island as often as we wished, so we brought the LADY JEANNE down to Jamesport's East Creek for a month before leaving for Maine. During that time we lived aboard, working hard at the nursery, but enjoying every morning and evening in a peaceful marsh-bordered creek, sandy beach nearby, only minutes from our work.

JAMESPORT TO MAINE ... OCTOBER-NOVEMBER 1978

September had been lovely in our secure creek, but October brought a fierce hurricane. We listened to Coast Guard reports of ships lost at sea; were we being irrational, planning to cruise to Maine so late in the year? Day after day the wind howled. All was in readiness ... we waited.

Saturday, October 7, more of the same. Suddenly, silence. It was already 5:00 P.M. No matter, we could wait no longer. We would make a dash for Shelter Island. We cast off our dock lines in Jamesport and scooted out into Peconic Bay, racing darkness. An hour and forty minutes later, sun long set behind us, water black before us, we groped our way into Dering Harbor and picked up our mooring. We were on our way!

Morning brought more wind. Would it never stop? We spent a bouncy Sunday, waves from the hurricane still pounding in. By Monday we were more than a little frustrated. It was still blustery, but by eleven-thirty we convinced ourselves that it must be moderating; besides, didn't we have a new, seagoing boat? Off we went, completely disregarding the fact that the sun sets before six in October.

We pushed the throttle up to 1900 rpm, and held it there until 5:38 p.m. when we passed the R "4" Red Bell near Cuttyhunk Island and about three miles inside the Buzzards Bay Entrance Light. My log shows no entry for time as we passed R "6", and after that darkness overtook us; I couldn't see well enough to tell the time; and I dared not switch on a light and interfere with our night vision. Behind us, no blazing sunset lingered to light the evening, only a grey oppressiveness. Ahead, to the east, blackness, punctuated by what seemed like hundreds of fireflies: lights, many colors, heights and frequencies. We were still about 23 miles away from our Onset anchorage. It had been years since we had cruised in the dark, and then, only in a very familiar harbor. Buzzards Bay after dark was a completely different kettle of fish.

I turned on the compass light and Joe reduced throttle. Then I went below with the chart and a flashlight to see if I could discern a light pattern that would help us find our way in. Sure enough, all of the lights to starboard in the canal approach were red, flashing every four seconds, up to the Cleveland East Ledge Light. Once in the Hog Island Channel the red lights alternated four and six seconds. That should help.

Joe concentrated on holding to the compass heading and I peered ahead into the hostile night, watching for obstacles. It seemed to take forever, but finally we rounded dolphin "11" which marks the entrance to Onset Bay.

While running a compass course we avoided using our search light, fearing the loss of our night vision and the possibility of confusing other voyagers. In the channel, however, our high-powered beautiful chrome two-mile spotlight would earn its keep for the first time. Joe switched on the light, grasped the handle and turned it toward the channel. A brilliant beam cut the darkness, then vanished almost instantly. Joe swore vehemently and I rushed forward up onto the trunk cabin to investigate. I found our elegant spotlight laying face down on the wheelhouse roof, its light illuminating only the circle on which it lay. It was only disconnected--not broken--but that was NOT the time to fix it. I went below and got a trusty Ever-ready, then went forward to sit shivering on the trunk cabin as I scanned the inky water for channel markers. In a few minutes we located a mooring. Safe at last. That twenty-three miles had taken three hours instead of the usual two; it was already eight-thirty. That was an inauspicious beginning, even for us. We would have to plan shorter days!

Tuesday dawned with more gusty wind. We took on 90 gallons of fuel, then returned to our Onset mooring to spend the day reading, walking and planning.

Wednesday we woke to a hazy day, but the weatherman said it would clear. We were so elated to see the wind lessened that even fog could not discourage us. We cast off at 6:25 A.M. and crept through Onset Bay Channel to the Cape Cod Canal. This time we turned on our radiotelephone, got well over to starboard and idled through the patchy fog. Someone was jogging on the path which borders the canal and we waved to him as he came and went in the mist; we prayed the fog would soon lift, but it was 8:50 A.M. before we could really see.

We advanced the throttle to 1900 rpm as we passed the Cape Cod BW Bell "CC". The day cleared into a frisky, blue water day and we made good time past Boston and around Cape Ann. We planned to reach Portsmouth

Harbor that day but, as we advanced toward Gunboat Shoal which marks the harbor entrance, the seas grew steeper and steeper. We had never entered Portsmouth before and didn't want to chance it in that sea. We retreated to Gosport Harbor on the Isles of Shoals.

A lobsterman was on his way out just as we were entering that harbor of refuge. We hailed him to inquire about a safe anchorage and he advised us to pick up his very heavy mooring, since he was bringing his boat to the mainland for the winter. There were no signs of life on those barren islands, just bare rock, old weatherbeaten houses, and scrubby growth. Not one person! We hosed the boat quickly and hurried ashore.

As the tide dropped the sheltered harbor became glassy smooth, reflecting the many-eyed houses, the grey rocks and the somber sky. It seemed an appropriate setting for a mystery and, indeed, a murder had once taken place there! We took a long ramble ashore and I gathered a pail of rose-hips which I made into jelly that evening.

The next day was warm and sunny; we explored and sunbathed in a sheltered nook and had a picnic. We felt so alone and peaceful we were reluctant to leave, but we decided that while it was clear and calm we should scoot across to Portsmouth Harbor. At 4:00 P.M. we cast off and we rounded Fort Point just after five.

This large and busy harbor is home to a navy yard which specializes in submarines, so it is wise to keep a sharp lookout in approaching the mouth of the Piscataqua River. We checked the cruising guide to find the way to Dion's Yacht Yard; though we had been there by car, going by sea is something else. Portsmouth Harbor is just a little jog on a car map; on a navigational chart it is an exciting array of coves, creeks, channels, bridges, islands and navigational aids. I would like to spend a month there in a small boat someday.

Dion's is located in Back Channel behind Seavey Island.We hailed someone in the yard and they directed us to a mooring we could use.We had to go around a couple of times to catch it, though, since the current was so strong. It was almost dark by the time we were settled, so we just made supper and had a quiet evening.

Friday morning we went ashore early to meet with Dion's yard foreman. We wanted to see if there was any inside winter storage space left and, also, to get an estimate for painting the boat. He came aboard to work up an estimate, but could not help with storage: they were all booked up for that winter. We started to worry. Here we were planning to store the boat in Maine ... what if no one had room for us! We decided to call Southwest Boat (in SW Harbor), to inquire if they still had room.

That evening, just after dusk, we set out for a row, not expecting to get too far in the swift current. We passed under one bridge and then started looking for a place to land so we could take a walk. The shores did not offer any landing places and we were ready to give up when we spotted a picnic table set up in a grassy, parklike area on the left bank. We agreed that it looked like 'public' property so we nosed in, clambered up some rocks, and tied the dinghy to a tree. Hand in hand we set off to explore; perhaps we could find some place to eat.

We strolled down a quiet, dark street which soon led to a well-lit gate house. It looked like the entrance to a military installation. We surmised that we wouldn't be able to go any farther that way and were about to retrace our steps when a young naval officer came out of the gate house to inform us that we were (already) in a restricted area. He asked how we had gotten IN without a pass. We told him we had landed in our dinghy and walked in, that we were unaware that this area was restricted (all very true). There had been no sign on the shore. This is hard to believe, I know, but that young man (probably from Ohio or Kansas) asked in all seriousness:

"What's a din-gee?"

We told him it was a small rowboat which we towed behind our cabin cruiser, and that we had come ashore in search of a restaurant.

"Well," he said, "you'd better get right back to your 'din-gee' and get out of here before anyone else catches you. You can tie up near the bridge on the north side of the channel and walk to some restaurants from there."

Picturing ourselves clapped in irons we made a hasty retreat, rowed across the channel and soon found another place to land, walked a bit, and found a pizza parlor crowded with friendly navy yard workers. They were a jolly group and we were soon recounting our recent adventure, to their great amusement. I hope security has been tightened since then!

Saturday morning we were up early and ready to head "down east." We cast off at 7:30 A.M. and by eight-fifteen were in sight of the "24YL" whistle off York Ledge, but the going was too rough: the seas were straight into us and, after climbing up and surfing down ever higher mountains, we decided to turn back.

We checked the cruising guide again and found that the Kittery Point Yacht Club maintains guest moorings in Pepperell Cove; we found the club, they had moorings available, and we were made welcome. That evening we had a delicious dinner in Captain Gideon's Galley on the second floor of the yacht club, and barely made it back to the LADY JEANNE. The wind and waves were so strong that Joe had all he could do to row us out. Our small outboard motor had been safely stowed in the bilge thus far, since Joe preferred to row; we took it out and put it on the dinghy. In these rough waters we might be unable to get back if we had to row any distance.

By evening the storm moved off and a beautiful full moon rose over Gooseberry Island. I called Joe out to share it and even took a picture which captured the moment. I remember wishing on the moon ... for calmer waters!

On Monday a sparkling autumn day greeted us; we were underway by seven. At seven-twenty we left Kitts Rocks to port, pushed the throttle to 1900 rpm and barrelled past York Ledge, Cape Porpoise, Cape Elizabeth and across Casco Bay. It was just 1:00 P.M. when we pulled in close to Seguin Island. There was a Coast Guard mooring to the east of the island and we were hoping it would be empty this late in the season, in which case our plan was to pick it up and visit the island. Unfortunately, it was already occupied, so we took a couple of pictures of water that was never more brilliant and Seguin wearing early fall colors, then bore on for the Sisters.

We passed the Cat Ledges at the mouth of the Sheepscot River and Hendricks Head, then cut behind Macmahan Island through the Goose Rocks Passage, following the directions supplied by the Cruising Guide. We soon found the marina at Riggs Cove on the Sasanoa River, picked up one of the empty moorings, and went ashore to find everything locked up tight. Safe in a cozy harbor, surrounded by thick woods clothed in red and gold, we walked for hours, saw not one person, and did not find any village. By the time we returned to the boat it felt like winter. In order to operate our two electric heaters we had to run the generator all evening. Fortunately, there was no one there to be annoyed by the noise ... just us.

We had installed an oil burner in the bow while building LADY JEANNE, but that was not an acceptable solution. It threw soot all over the boat, required a high stack to provide adequate draft, and needed the generator to run the AC motor. After that, we had tried a bulkhead-mounted kerosene stove, but that also let us down. When it went out, it did not automatically shut off the fuel. We came back one day to find the cushion beneath the stove soaked with stove oil. We still had not solved the problem of adequate heat that would not need a noisy generator.

When we were finished with dinner and our baths we shut off the generator and, well bundled against the chilling air, we curled up together on the back deck under millions of stars. There was not one light anywhere ashore but, the sun's light, bounced off a full moon, cast a golden highway across the wondrously motionless water. We could have been the only people on earth. We slept like exhausted children in that pristine haven, bunks piled high with quilts, the only sound an occasional muted bird call.

The sun was already well up in the sky when a persistent little buzzing woke me: a mosquito had sneaked in and was trying to find breakfast. We looked out to discover a perfect day for the trip we had planned. Having read about the inside passage from Boothbay Harbor to Bath in the CRUISING GUIDE TO THE NEW ENGLAND COAST, we were eager to tackle it. The authors had described it as "one of the most delightful trips on the coast ... the passage ... narrow, crooked, and with strong tidal currents."

After a bountiful breakfast and a lazy morning it was already 12:45 P.M. before we cast off. First, we ran all the way into Robinhood Cove where an abandoned coasting schooner lay, framed by crimson and gold trees. Here and there a cottage snuggled against the shores. Then, north through Knubble Bay and past Beal Island, where the fabled Lower Hell Gate awaited us. Current velocities up to 9.0 knots have been observed there near The Boilers; 3.0 knots on the flood and 3.5 knots on the ebb are usual. This makes the twisted strait extremely hazardous for small boats and sailing vessels. We had plenty of power, but we had to steer very accurately to avoid the dangerous rocks, eddies and whirlpools. We had studied the area carefully and were at full attention as we entered the narrow passage. At that moment a big Coast Guard cutter (the first boat we had seen that day) started through from the other end. Moving at a good clip, a speed adequate to maintain steerage in the swift current, he bore down upon us. Unable to simply stop and wait in the wild, rockbound passage, adrenaline flowing, we maintained our heading and passed within feet of the speeding vessel. Whew! That was close!

Next, we pulled into Hockamock Bay, absolutely beautiful in its autumn dress. We did have some difficulty keeping to the deep water in the narrow channel. We continued past Hockamock Point into the Sasanoa River and the Upper Hell Gate, even more narrow but less swift; then, on through Hanson Bay and under a fixed bridge. (51' vert. cl.) into the powerful Kennebec River. We crossed the river near the Route I vertical lift bridge and waved to workers who were climbing over navy ships being built or repaired at Bath Iron Works.

Joe at the helm. Behind him, the vertical lift bridge at Bath, Maine.
October 17, 1978.

The passage which we had just negotiated was long on excitement but short on distance, only 11 nautical miles. It was just two-fifteen. We decided to retrace that beautiful route back to the Sheepscot River. The second time we enjoyed it more, since we weren't so nervous. We savored the scenery and took several pictures. Back at Riggs Cove we went through the Little Sheepscot River (instead of Goose Rocks Passage), past Turnip Island then through the tiny passage at Five Islands. What a magnificent spot this is, the islands standing up like jewels against the bright water of Sheepscot Bay.

We crossed Sheepscot River to Green Island, then Ebenecook Harbor to Cameron Point, and went through a very narrow opening to Townsend Gut, a shortcut to Boothbay Harbor. The swing bridge opened quickly when we sounded our horn, and the tender asked for the name of our yacht and of the skipper. They must have quite a list by now.

Once in Boothbay Harbor we found Pierce's Marine on the east side of the inner harbor, took on 95 gallons of fuel, washed down the boat, and then picked up one of their moorings. It was almost dark when we set off on foot for downtown Boothbay, about a forty minute walk when one crosses on the footbridge. The town was much quieter than it is in the summer, very pleasant. We climbed the steps to the Ebb Tide Restaurant and, to our surprise, found a Maine friend, Walter Leighton.

Walter is the yard foreman and senior mechanic at Southwest Boat Corporation where our fuel and water tanks had been manufactured. He and his wife, Hilda, also own the Harbor Light Tourist Home, where we had stayed very comfortably when we came up to supervise construction of the LADY JEANNE.

We joined him and ordered a haddock dinner, then recounted our plans to store the boat in Maine, return to New York until after Christmas, then move to Maine permanently. He was the very man who could help us on all counts. Fortunately, he could affirm the availability of boat storage space at Southwest Boat, and he and Hilda would save a couple of adjoining rooms; when we moved up, we'd have a place to stay while we looked for a house or apartment to rent. What a relief!

FIVE ISLANDS, MAINE.
Passage lies between beacon and rock.

The next morning we took the dinghy down to the town dock and browsed around town before shopping for fresh food. We try to alternate our overnight stops: if we spend one night in a lonely, deserted anchorage, the next night we aim for a village with some services and opportunities for sociability. After Boothbay, we would want a peaceful harbor.

We cast off at 3:00 P.M., went across Linekin Bay, through Fisherman Island Passage and into the mouth of the Damariscotta River. It was just four o'clock when we left the red and white beacon close to starboard and entered picturesque Christmas Cove on Rutherford Island.

This is a favorite stopover for cruising men and we would never go there in high summer, but on October 18th it was completely deserted. We quickly found a vacant guest mooring (white spars with red tops), and were on our way to enjoy the sunset from the top of the ridge overlooking the harbor and Johns Bay. A lone fisherman was still hauling traps in The Thread of Life, a tiny, rockbound passage on the east side of the island. The fort on Pemaquid Point was just visible in the gathering dusk. Every summer service was shut up tight for the winter, and we encountered no sign of life during our long ramble.

It was dark and cold when we got back to the boat. We ran the generator, turned on the heaters and made dinner, but we would almost rather have gone cold and hungry than disturb the perfect peace with that noisy motor. The sky was beautiful, but it was too cold to stay up in the wheelhouse; protected only by canvas curtains, it cooled right off after sunset. Regretfully, we went below and closed the hatch.

A few drops of rain were falling from a cloudy sky when we abandoned Christmas Cove just before ten the next morning. We crossed Johns Bay and cleared Pemaquid Ledge, then crossed Muscongus Bay and poked into Port Clyde for the first time. Outside Mosquito Island a following sea raced us to the Muscle Ridge Channel. What a sleigh ride! We crossed West Penobscot Bay to McIntosh Ledge; here, we could see the Camden Hills across water that was now flat calm. How many changes each day brings in Maine.

Up East Penobscot Bay to Cape Rosier and into Eggemoggin Reach (put away chart 13302). It was just three-ten when we rounded Green Ledge off Western Island. At that point, navigation became very confusing. We had a new chart of the area (13309), but all the numbers on the buoys off Little Deer Isle had been changed. Fortunately, it was calm and we got into the Reach, passed under the Deer Isle Bridge, and at 4:25 P.M. were picking up a mooring in Center Harbor. The town of Brooklin is just a mile from the harbor and, while there, we visited the old headquarters of WOODEN-BOAT MAGAZINE, shopped at the Brooklin General Store and studied the boats in Joel White's boatyard.

The next day we made an uneventful passage to Bass Harbor ... HOME! It was just October 21, so could harbor-hop on Mount Desert Island for three lovely weeks.

After spending a couple of days in Bass Harbor (checking our little house, visiting Mildred and Bobby), we moved to a mooring in Southwest Harbor where we visited Ralph Stanley's boat shop. Ralph had built many fine friendship sloops and lobster boats, and we wanted to check out his workmanship.

This was not just idle curiosity. By this time we were seriously thinking of building another new boat if we could sell the LADY JEANNE at a decent price. We loved the boat and had enjoyed our trips in her, but if we were really going to live in Maine we would need an enclosed wheelhouse, adequate, safe and quiet heat, and insulated glass. We thought about altering LJ but realized it was not practical; better to start over, to design in the changes we felt necessary for a long boating season in this colder climate.

We took Eric Edwards, owner of Southwest Boat Corporation, out to inspect the LADY JEANNE, and asked him to begin looking for a buyer. Then we moved to a Manset mooring where the view of Somes Sound and the mountains is unsurpassed. Rocky Homer at the Boathouse willingly loaned us her car so we could run to Bass Harbor where our mail awaited us.

It was getting very rough in Manset and, after a couple of rainy days, we made a dash for Bass Harbor across the turbulent bar from Great Gott Island. If it was going to be nasty, we might as well work on our house.

We picked up a mooring in Bass Harbor and then spent three days tearing out stairs and building a wall along the driveway of our little house. When the weather improved we returned to Southwest Harbor, where we showed the boat to a couple of local yacht brokers. On the second of November we cruised down Somes Sound on a day so warm that we donned bathing suits to get a little more tan before winter set in.

All of the summer facilities were closed and getting water began to be a problem; we had to resort to lobster docks to fill our tanks, and they were usually busy and not too hospitable to pleasure boats who only wanted something for nothing. We took on 92 gallons of fuel at Beal's Dock, but their dock water line had already been shut off for the winter.

We ran over to Northeast Harbor hoping to find water at their town dock. There, we hailed the mission boat, SUNBEAM, and her skipper, David Allen, told us to come alongside and tie to the SUNBEAM, since the only open water tap was near his slip. We filled our tanks, had a good visit, and spent the night in a Northeast Harbor that no summer visitor would recognize.

LADY JEANNE tied to SUNBEAM in NORTHEAST HARBOR

Back in Southwest Harbor we lived aboard until one morning when we woke to find the boat covered with ice. We felt that for safety's sake this must be the end of living aboard. We rented a room at the Harbor Light and shopped the BAR HARBOR TIMES for an inexpensive car to carry us back to New York. We stayed to watch our treasure lifted from the water and stored inside. On November 17, we were back at work in the nursery ... counting the days now till we could move to Maine.

At Thanksgiving time we drove to Pittsburgh with Paul and Marie; she was to be godmother to her namesake, Marie Sorensen, Michele's new baby. The kids stayed in Michele's house, but Joe and I went to the Holiday Inn where a terrific band was playing.We danced until almost three in the morning, and drove the 500 miles home with agonizing headaches. Like the night in Camden's Bay Street Garage, we agreed that the memory was worth the pain. We have gone for years at a time with our minds and hearts firmly set on being responsible parents and hard-working, sober citizens. But once in a while ...

After an exciting family Christmas we began the task of packing up. We would go to Maine with only a car-full: Joe, Paul and I, and our most valued treasures. Our pictures, books, handmade rugs and quilts, favorite dishes and pots, linens, clothes and color television were included. More bulky treasures were stored in the attic. Every time we came to New York to check the nursery we would take another load to Maine.

Our apartment above the nursery was made ready for our daughter Jeanne, her husband Chris, and baby Beth. They had been living in the large farmhouse Chris' grandparents used in the summer, but the cost of fuel was undermining their budget. Chris was trying to establish himself in the piano tuning and repair business; they were struggling. We offered them the apartment in exchange for some care-taking and home maintenance of the nursery buildings and grounds, an arrangement we hoped would help Jeanne while keeping our properties safe from vandalism as well as the nursery well groomed.

1979

On January 5, I gave the keys to the nursery to Marie Burding, our head teacher and new manager, kissed everyone goodbye, waved to the children at every window, and began the happy journey to a new life in Maine. This was a real turning point in my life. I had been caring for children since I was five years old: my five younger siblings, our own nine and in recent years two thousand of other people's children in the nursery. It would be strange having only one adolescent in the house. I would miss my career in child care but I had to admit that I had done "my thing."

Now it was time for a change. Joe had been fighting depression for over two years and was still taking antidepressant drugs. While he was steadily improving, he could not stand pressure.

Once in Maine we stayed at the Harbor Light for two weeks until we found a furnished efficiency apartment. It was cozy, but I really wanted to keep hens and have a garden. We found a small furnished house in Bass Harbor just around the block from our own little Ferry Road house.

Paul went off to Mount Desert Island High School where he was soon involved in a marvelous production of THE WIZ, making friends and discovering hitherto unrealized talents for drawing and painting in Mrs. Holmbom's art classes.

Eric Edwards showed LADY JEANNE to Bill Moore of Orcutt Harbor and he made an offer contingent on a successful sea trial to take place in mid-April. Since we knew the boat performed perfectly we could relax and enjoy our first winter in Maine.

We visited every boat builder on Mount Desert and in the surrounding communities, hiked beautiful mountain trails, skated on the glistening ice of hidden lakes, and chauffeured Paul home from play practice almost every evening. A very different but memorable season.

On April 18, the LADY JEANNE was launched and we took a shake-down cruise to Cranberry Isles; we were ready for our prospective buyer. Bill Moore came aboard the next day to take the boat for a run; he was satisfied and said he would take it. No money had yet changed hands, but Eric assured us the deal would go through.

We made a quick trip to Center Harbor to show Joel White this LADY JEANNE so he would have a better idea of the kind of boat we wanted; we had just about decided that he would build our next boat.

The check came. We said farewell to our lovely, cherished boat and closed one of the most exciting chapters in our life together. As always, when we turn a corner, we do not look back ...

8

ZOBEL SEA FOX
1966 ... 24'

"POPOVER"
Power: Buick 350 gas

In 1961 when we traveled through Maine while building the Clayton Fletcher boat, we fell in love with the peaceful "Pine Tree State." Very tempted to move, we looked at farmhouses and wrote to several realtors, but at that time we had eight children, the oldest only twelve. We were afraid we would find it difficult to make a living in Maine and that opportunities would be too limited for our bright children.

When I started the day care center in 1966, that entailed a commitment which was to fill our lives for thirteen years. Meanwhile, our love of the natural world was satisfied through long boating seasons which also enabled us to spend wonderful hours with our young family. We still had to earn Maine.

We named our business PINE TREE DAY NURSERY, INC. On the wall in my office I hung a picture that always reminded me of our Maine dream: a quiet cove, fringed with spruce clad mountains, a red roofed cabin snuggled on the shore. When we finally made the move we were choosing a quality of life and voting with our feet. Maine is not perfect, but there is lots of land and only about a million people. That makes all the difference. Progress has left ugly scars here as everywhere, and there are even some toxic waste dump sites, but as you drive Route 95 from Kittery to Bangor you see nothing but trees. I was determined that I would own my own trees as soon as possible. But first, a new boat!

Our first winter as Maine residents was spent visiting all the boat builders in the area. We realized that if we wanted a fine boat we would have to hire a highly skilled builder with a hard working crew who would pay close attention to details without wasting time. When we found Joel White in Brooklin, and looked at the boats he had already built for others, we knew our search was ended.

At the time he was finishing a lobster boat and had a full year of other work scheduled. First, we had to interest him in the project, then be willing to wait until 1980 when he could start a boat for us.

Once again, we refused to spend a year without a boat. We started looking for a small craft to fill our lives while we waited. Locating a small cruising boat in Maine is much more difficult than in New York or Connecticut where there are thousands from which to choose. Here, we found just a few boats available, most of them old wooden lobster boats with iron fastenings bleeding rust, sorry old gas engines, and many scars from a life of hard work.

Then we happened upon POPOVER: a 24' Zobel Sea Fox. She was sitting pretty in Center Harbor, right off Joel White's Brooklin Boat Yard. We told Joel that it was just the kind of skiff we were looking for. While it wore no *for sale* sign, Joel thought it might possibly be available since it had hardly been used during the previous summer; the owner had been sick. Minutes later, a phone call to Arthur Wood had confirmed Joel's conjecture; we rowed out and climbed aboard.

Built in1966 of mahogany over oak, POPOVER had been given a new fresh water-cooled 350 Buick engine that had been run no more than thirty hours over about five years. It needed a good cleaning and a tune-up, but it should be reliable. The lapstrake hull was very sound. Joel White had himself replaced the worn deck canvas with dynel cloth and resin a few years before. This was done in good time to save the little boat from the usual fate of older wooden boats: fresh water leaks in the decks and resultant rot. She had two bunks, a head, and a canvas cockpit cover, our minimum requirements.

We could not understand why anyone would give a boat such a strange name. Later, we found that the boat's first owner had been a Mount Desert Island native who had borrowed the name from a local restaurant's most famous specialty. For 132 years the Jordan Pond House had been known the world over for its "Tea and Popovers," served in the elegant manner of a bygone era, a tradition that was interrupted when the building was destroyed by fire on June 24, 1979. (A beautiful new Pond House opened in 1982.)

We drove to Arthur's house and talked money. He wanted $5,000 for POPOVER and was quite firm since the engine was so new. That was really more than we had hoped to spend, but the choices were so limited, it was the middle of May, and we could not imagine a summer without a boat. We finally agreed on a price of $4,500, without the trailer.

On May 23rd when we rode POPOVER home to Bass Harbor, we found her to be a dry, comfortable and able little craft. We were well pleased with her performance, considering her size.

Joe cleaned the bilges, serviced the engine, installed a new head (how many heads have we bought to date?) and bolted a new two-burner propane stove to the top of the engine box. I washed cabin and cushions, hung towel rods and wash basins, and set up housekeeping. We were soon ready to do some local cruising.

POPOVER; flag flying, coffee on and music playing.

To find out what I mean by "local" cruising you might go to your local boating supply store and ask to see chart 13313: Approaches to Blue Hill Bay, and 13318: Frenchman Bay and Mount Desert Island. Even if you never come to Maine, these charts would make beautiful decorations for any seaman's den. They are the stuff of which dreams are made. Talk about cruising! Talk about islands!

Within an hour or two in any direction from our mooring in Bass Harbor we had cruising to last a lifetime: coves, islands, bays, reaches, and rivers, all surrounded by the cleanest, coldest water imaginable, in sight of the ever lovely and constantly changing Mount Desert Range. Only the hardiest of swimmers brave this water, and falling overboard can be fatal. In many ways we found it more fun to have a small boat in Maine: we could explore many places which we would avoid with a big, expensive boat; we could anchor in isolated, peaceful hideaways. Every day held a new adventure.

Since we still owned the day nursery and many of our children lived on Long Island, New York trips were still quite frequent. In February we went down for Renee's wedding, and in July we made another visit to see the family and check our nursery. It was still surviving quite well without us; our capable staff was stretching and growing with their new responsibilities.

On that trip we brought my mother back for a Maine visit which included boat rides, car tours, berry picking and hiking. It was fun sharing the wonders of our new home with her. On one cruise with mother, the fog closed in as we neared the buoy marking Western Way. We had to creep back to Southwest Harbor and wait for it to lift, then try again. Mother remained calm through the eerie ordeal, but she later confided that she had really been worried. I know the feeling. Fog is an ever present possibility in Maine; it can sweep in so suddenly, especially in July and August. For this reason, we always run compass courses even in very familiar waters on clear days.

After using POPOVER for a few weeks, we suddenly realized that we were smelling gas. The gas tanks and lines were new, connections tight, where was the gas leaking? With the floor boards and engine cover raised we ran the engine and discovered a very fine spray of gas coming from a pin hole leak in the fuel filter. We replaced the automobile filter with a good marine fuel filter. Using auto parts on boats is the worst kind of economy; the boat could have been lost, not to mention lives!

In August, son Paul went away to camp at Pilgrim Lodge with some new friends. Joe and I took advantage of his absence to plan several weekends-a-deux in surrounding harbors. On one such mini-vacation we were anchored in Center Harbor on a rainy afternoon when a speedboat appeared out of the fog carrying our son Jim and his wife, Gail. They had been bike touring in the area and realizing that we were also in that neighborhood had sought out the harbor and looked for us. Once they spotted our boat it was only a few minutes before they had locked their bikes and found an obliging youngster to bring them out. (In Maine, there is always someone who will be helpful.)

We cooked a jolly supper together and they bedded down under our cockpit cover for a more comfortable night than they would have had camping in the rain. While living in Bass Harbor we made our home available to our visiting children even when we were boating and always left a note giving our general plans. This was one time our foresight had paid off with a pleasant visit.

We spent the first weekend in September anchored in Somesville Harbor watching a pair of osprey raise a family on Bar Island. We hiked and picnicked on that jewel-like island which belongs to Acadia National Park.

On our way back down Somes Sound the boat suddenly stopped moving forward, though the engine was still running fine. I looked over the stern and saw pink foam gushing out of the exhaust pipes. That was a new one for me, but Joe realized at once that the pink had to be transmission fluid leaking from somewhere! We poured a couple of quarts of engine oil into the transmission and were able to move forward again. (We always carry enough oil to re-fill the system, but this was the only time we used our reserve.) We limped down the sound fearing that at any moment we would stop again, but we made it to a Boathouse mooring off the Manset shore.

Joe started taking things apart and soon determined that the transmission oil cooler was leaking. He removed the strange, old-fashioned part and we rowed ashore. After walking to the main intersection about a mile distant, we hitch-hiked to our home in Bass Harbor. When we called the Boathouse the next morning (Monday) we were relieved to learn that we could use the mooring since many summer visitors had already gone. We rented it for a month and resolved to enjoy that harbor while getting the boat operational again. The view from Manset is striking: mountains looming over Somes Sound, islands silhouetted against the bright Atlantic, fiery sunsets over Western Mountain and unobstructed moon risings over East Bunker Ledge. The Moorings (a shore restaurant) advertises it as a billion dollar view. Here, too, inflation has taken its toll; it used to be called a million dollar view!

We took the leaking part to the Power and Robinson Machine Shop in Bass Harbor and they promised they could get a replacement in a few days. Joe drained the transmission thoroughly to make sure all the heavy engine oil was out, installed the new part, and we were operational again. I'm thankful he is such a capable mechanic; with older boats there always seems to be something needing repair. I take that back. With ANY boats!

Though the nights were getting quite cold in September, we hated to end the overnight cruises. We brought our trusty Aladin (brand name, not mis-spelling) kerosene heater aboard. We never left it running once we were ready to sleep, but it did keep the boat cozy during the evenings, and Joe would get up first in the morning, light the fire and put the kettle on. By the time I woke up the boat was warm, Joe already shaved, and my wash water boiling. Any space heater can be dangerous and especially so on a boat. We screwed ours down to the deck and never lit it while running or when the sea was less than perfectly calm.

During the last weekend in September we anchored in the lee of Black Island, spent the night alone under the stars, and hiked the rocky shores and deer trails. Now deserted, that island was once the site of a bustling quarry operation. In the rubble near an old dig we found an ancient wooden toy airplane; a copy of Lindberg's monoplane "The Spirit of St. Louis."

We also found several sections of an old shed which had washed ashore on the beach. As I had long been planning to keep a few hens to supply our own eggs; I realized the boards we could salvage from that old shed would make the building of a hen house less expensive. Joe and I got to work with hammers and crow bars. Soon we had the nails pulled from a pile of usable boards. We loaded the dinghy and rowed to POPOVER with our treasure. We returned to the island for two more loads before we had all the good material salvaged. This was the first of our boats to double as a mini coastal freighter.

Had I been a man, I'm sure I would have been a carpenter like my father, and I was still hoping to help build my own house some day. A hen house might not seem like much of a building, but it was one of the most satisfying experiences of my life: planning, measuring, sawing and nailing. First on any tour of our little house is "the hen house I built!" I did have to buy tar paper and chicken wire, but it was still a mighty thrifty project. I bought five mature hens from our egg lady (Christine Gilley, fine Maine artist and good friend), and our daughter Marie gave us four more biddies when we went home for Christmas. They rode in a big box and laid two eggs enroute. Our flock of nine hens has averaged two dozen eggs each week and they eat all our food wastes. The raccoons never bother our trash cans. Hens are the most efficient re-cyclers, turning food scraps, worms, garden wastes, weeds and grain into high quality protein, a perfect food, the egg! You have never tasted a good poached egg until you have kept your own hens.

On October 29th we took our last ride around the islands, and then hauled POPOVER at Jim Rich's boat yard in West Tremont. In November, Paul acted the part of Slender in Shakespeare's MERRY WIVES OF WINDSOR (a great show!). We spent Thanksgiving with my brother John and his family at their home near Augusta, and went to New York for Christmas. The year had brought us two new granddaughters: Shoshanna Young, born to Jeanne in June, and April Thompson, born to Renee in August. A very good year!

1980

On January 6th we celebrated our personal New Years Day. It was just one year since we had moved to Maine. We agreed that the decision had been prudent: Joe's depression seemed to be behind him and Paul was happier in school than he had ever been previously.

I began the new year right by applying for a lobster and crab fishing license and started looking for a few second hand traps. One lady sold me five old traps which had been taking up room in her barn at five dollars each; then I bought three better traps from a Coast Guardsman who was moving, for eight dollars apiece. In the coming year we would add crabs and lobsters to our foraged food which already included mussels, clams, mackerel, raspberries, blueberries, blackberries, cranberries and apples. With our hens and a thriving vegetable garden we were moving toward a down-east self-sufficiency.

This was fun for me, but also quite necessary. We had banked the money from the sale of the Bobby Rich boat (except for the price of a 1973 Comet since our old red Ford would no longer pass inspection), but we knew that the inflation rate would make our new boat more expensive. Since our income from the day care center was very modest, we had to practice every possible economy to avoid unmanageable new debt. When the new boat was finished, POPOVER would be sold, if not at a profit, at least for close to what she had cost.

During the first year we owned POPOVER we had installed a new compass, cabin and deckhouse lights, a starter switch and two fire extinguishers in addition to the new head, fuel filter and transmission oil cooler. Since we had bought her in the water and kept her until November we had not done any painting during that first year. As soon as the weather warmed in April, Joe got to work: scraping, sanding and painting. He also took out the rusty exhaust pipes and installed mufflers and new pipes in an effort to quiet that big, noisy engine. Our improvements had cost $800 in cash plus lots of hours of our own labor, but POPOVER looked great when we launched in May.

We painted our lobster buoys Chesapeake green using paint left over from our Nevins, and set our traps. We would fish them every two or three days, but we used the boat almost every day. On sunny days we often anchored just behind Lopaus Point to lie in the sun, have lunch and read the papers. Sometimes we would take the boat over to Brooklin to monitor the progress on the new boat.

On one such trip we got caught in the fog in Casco Passage. We held to our course with painstaking care and found our way from buoy to buoy. Suddenly, a ship's bell sounded in the gloom and the cruise schooner VICTORY CHIMES emerged from the fog under full sail, her radar spinning confidently. Her captain obviously knew where we were, but we were truly surprised at that ghostly materialization. To our great relief we cleared Black Island and found the CP Bell without running aground, but soon another challenge arose.

Out in the open water of Blue Hill Bay a brisk wind from the west promised to take out the fog but the water was leaping; we were in for a rough crossing. For no obvious reason a red light flashed on our dash board signalling "TILT"! That message was obsolete: there was nothing to tilt on the boat! What was causing the red light to operate? There must be a short circuit somewhere.

Under normal conditions we would have stopped immediately to look for the trouble, but we dared not. In that wind we would soon be swept off our course into the reefs and ledges off Swans Island. Our best hope lay in keeping to our course at least until the visibility improved. Somehow we made it back to Bass Harbor. Both of us were exhausted from the tension, fearful that the boat might explode at any moment.

As we tied POPOVER to her mooring a puff of smoke escaped from between the floor boards near the helm. I grabbed the fire extinguisher and Joe began unscrewing the floor boards. I really felt like running for my life, but I couldn't leave Joe and he was always so sure he could cope with whatever situation we encountered. He lifted the floor board to find a determined little flame working away at it. We doused the flame and looked for the cause of the fire; it was not hard to find. A floor frame had been routed out to permit passage of two wires from the helm to the starter. The floor board which lay over this frame was somewhat warped so that it set up a constant rattle. A few days before, Joe had determined to get rid of that annoying noise, and had put a couple of screws into the board. You guessed it; one of the screws went right between the wires. Another almost fatal lesson. Is there no end to the lessons boating people must learn?

On June 27th, our new boat was launched. POPOVER became a "has been." We listed her with the local brokers, but she had a lonely summer on her mooring in Southwest Harbor. We used her to set our lobster traps and I often rowed over to fish for mackerel from her cockpit. When Michele and her family came to Maine for a month we took them fishing on POPOVER. The new boat was definitely NOT a fishing boat!

Early in September, Tom Emlen showed POPOVER to an older couple who wanted to watch birds on Somes Sound. They asked us to bring her to their Somes Sound boatyard so their mechanic could inspect her before they made a commitment. We made an appointment to meet the following day. In order to eliminate the transportation problem we decided to take both boats to that rendezvous. I ran the new LADY JEANNE and Joe took the little Zobel.

As we neared the dock at Cochran's Boatyard, Joe went well ahead of me making some gay, speedy circles in the water, showing off the boat for the prospective buyers who were standing there awaiting our arrival. Suddenly, the boat stopped dead and a cloud of white smoke billowed from under the engine box, almost obscuring the little craft. I didn't know what to do. Was Joe in danger? Should I get closer or keep clear?

I crept cautiously closer so we could shout to each other. We could not imagine what had happened; the boat had always run so well; the engine was really almost new. In dismay we watched our customers walking away. Up the ramp and gone forever, no doubt. And who could blame them. They had been ready to pay $4,000 for POPOVER, money we badly needed at that point. Did anyone ever have such terrible luck?

The smoke gradually cleared, and Tom rowed out to tow POPOVER to the dock. I picked up a mooring and rowed ashore to ascertain what had happened. It did not take long to discover that the boat had run out of gas. Joe had wanted to fill the tank that morning but I had vetoed that idea. Always thrifty, I could not see putting gas in a boat we were about to sell. I was sure we had enough to get down the sound, not allowing for any speed show, of course. When the gas ran out, the anti-freeze in the cooling system boiled over the engine. There was nothing wrong with the boat.

Tom explained the situation to his customers and they had their mechanic check everything. The sale went through after all. We said farewell to our eighth boat: a fine little craft that had given us countless happy memories.

The new owners changed her name to TINKERTOY and proceeded to run up a big bill at their boatyard by having the yard insulate the engine box and paint the whole boat, inside and out. Owning even a small boat can be expensive when the owners can't do their own work.

9

JOEL WHITE DOWNEAST CRUISER
1980 ... 42'

"LADY JEANNE"
Power: 671 General Motors Diesel

In April 1977 when Bobby Rich launched our third LADY JEANNE, we had thought it would be our last boat, but it seemed we had to try once more to build the perfect boat. Settled in Maine we'd had hundreds of boat builders to choose from, many of them right on Mount Desert Island.

We watched Bunker and Ellis build a 38' boat for a local lobsterman which turned out to be their last effort. Both in their seventies, they were unwilling to start another boat. Ralph Stanley was also at work on a 36' charter boat while Bobby Rich was finally building a boat for himself. Watching the three shops simultaneously working on similar projects was an invaluable education in the art of wooden boat construction.

Though we loved wooden boats, we had a brief flirtation with fiberglass. Lee Wilbur had just finished a pleasure cruiser for Curtis Blake on a 46' Jarvis Newman hull. It was very well done, and we considered having him build for us, using that hull and our specs. A trial ride on a fiberglass lobster boat, however, changed our minds. We just didn't like the ride; after all the years of wooden boats we were spoiled!

After seemingly endless study and thought, Joel White, Naval Architect and renowned wooden boat builder was finally selected as the designer-builder of our ninth (and hopefully last) boat. After the launching of the Rich boat in April 1979, our first and only cruise had taken us to Center Harbor, home of Joel's Brooklin Boatyard. Since the Rich boat had come close to epitomizing our dream of a perfect livaboard cruiser we wanted

Joel to incorporate the successful features in the new boat, while at the same time understanding and correcting those aspects which had failed.

Joel took our sketches and drew a set of plans based on the hull he had just designed for Duffy and Duffy. We bought another 671 General Motors Diesel engine and had it trucked to Brooklin.

I don't know if its possible to build a flawless boat which will satisfy anyone forever, but after owning eight, we felt we had learned enough to come close. Every decision we made during the planning and construction of the Joel White boat was based on previous experience and careful reasoning.

No two people think alike or have identical needs, so layout is largely a matter of personal preference. Construction, on the other hand, should adhere to proven standards of excellence if a boat is to deliver safe, comfortable performance and a long, trouble-free life. People with unlimited funds can afford costly mistakes; at that point we could not. The purchase of this boat was the largest investment of our lifetimes; it was possible only because of years of crowded living, shabby old cars, hand-me-down clothes, and careful budgeting. We hoped that this time we would do everything right!

Since we had lived aboard boats varying from 24' to 54' we had learned that a 42' boat with a 13'6" beam could best accommodate the comforts we felt essential, while keeping all costs at a minimum. By placing the main bulkhead at the exact center we had twenty-one feet forward, and the engine at the center of buoyancy flanked by the two fuel tanks for perfect balance.

The layout we designed included every feature we wanted for living

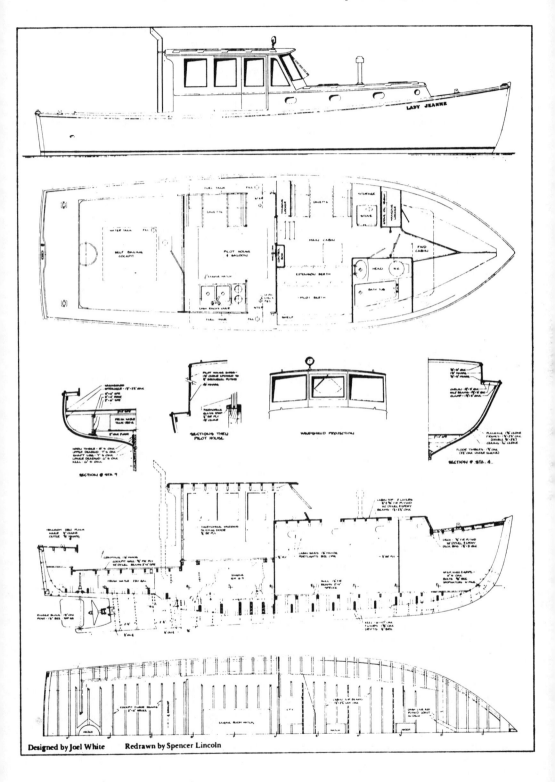

Designed by Joel White   **Redrawn by Spencer Lincoln**

aboard in comfort: sleeping for four in two separate compartments; a large bathroom with bathtub; two dinettes; a couch; an efficient galley; safe, economical heat and hot water; adequate light and ventilation; and well designed storage spaces. In spite of this long list of built-in furnishings we also wanted the boat to be spacious and uncluttered, with room for unrestricted movement, exercise and even dancing!

We utilized every inch of the forecastle by installing spacious vee berths, under which and all the way to the bow we located a large rope locker. The anchor rope was passed through a 4″ PVC pipe from under the berths to the foredeck where an Ideal windlass was installed. A hanging locker and spacious shelves provided adequate storage, while a full length mirror on the back of the door made grooming easy. Two opening ports and a Bomar hatch made this a comfortable, bright and airy stateroom.

The main cabin featured a Dickinson oil stove with oven for heat and winter cooking. The stove is drip-fed from a tank installed in the forward hanging locker. Next, to port, we put a cozy dinette for two which also functioned as my office, a good place for reading and bedtime snacks, as well as a cool mealtime retreat on hot days. It included space for magazines, file-boxes and a typewriter, and a bright reading light. A large, deep hanging locker completed the port side.

To starboard, we located the enclosed head which serves as a buffer between the two sleeping areas. We had Duffy and Duffy build us a four foot fiberglass bathtub which was built in enough above floor level to allow the water to drain without a sump pump. We also installed a hand shower for easy shampooing and a retractable clothes line above the tub to provide for the overnight drying of hand wash. I have never liked stainless steel sinks, so I insisted on a pretty oval Kohler porcelain sink which was built into a roomy teak storage cabinet with a good mirror and lights above.

Aft of the head there are two berths, both thirty inches wide, which I consider minimum for comfortable sleep. The top berth is fixed in the manner of pilot berths; the lower berth serves as a couch by day, but pulls out effortlessly to full width for sleeping. A locker, midships on the main bulkhead, encloses all the wiring and controls for accessible, stand-up servicing, as well as a good car stereo and cassette player. The two speakers were mounted over the hanging lockers in the main cabin. Six large opening portholes and another Bomar hatch provide excellent light and ventilation in this main cabin. Three steps with storage under lead up to the wheelhouse-salon.

The wheelhouse was divided for its three functions: engine operation, food preparation and dining. The helm is equipped with an eight inch card Danforth compass and central steering, both of which assist in accurate dead-reckoning navigation. It is flanked by two depth finders. These are the best insurance against grounding, as well as a help in navigation. They are hung above, where the navigator can watch them while seated at the dinette table with charts at hand. The ship-to-shore radio and spotlight are also hung above, out of the way but accessible. There is space to install a radar and other equipment in the future. The center window of the windshield opens out, and sliding doors to port and starboard make going forward to anchor safe and easy, as well as providing very controllable ventilation.

Aft to starboard there is a 5'6" galley and, to port, a 5'6" dinette which seats four. Center aft, a hinged door opens out to a 9'6" cockpit down one step from the wheelhouse. The stern is finished with a three foot aft deck where there is always a breeze for comfortable sunbathing. The open storage space under this deck is raised about three inches above the cockpit floor. Hefty bronze scuppers drain the cockpit.

The wheelhouse windows were custom-made by Soule of tempered, insulated glass, a feature which eliminates dripping windows. The galley includes a double sink by Kohler, 33" wide, just like the one I chose for my home. We kept a small dish drainer in one sink to eliminate the need for a drainboard. A two burner stainless steel gas stove by Paul Luke is located forward of the sink. Two Koolatron refrigerator units are built into drawers below, one on each side under silver and utensil drawers. A center galley locker under the sink and two large drawers under the dinette provide storage for food, dishes and pots.

An "on-demand" gas hot water heater by Kiley hangs on the aft bulkhead above the galley; this unit is the most sensible source of hot water I've seen, requiring no storage tank and costing very little to operate. Two ten-gallon aluminum gas storage tanks are stored outside under the coaming.

The entire interior of the LADY JEANNE is finished bright: captain's varnish gleaming on Bryunzeel mahogany bulkheads, fir flooring, cedar sealing, laminated oak stringers and carlings and locust corner posts. In spite of great temptation to varnish the fine mahogany on the exterior of the trunk and wheelhouse, we held to our original plan and painted the whole outside. Nothing protects wood from weather like good marine paint.

All decks are constructed of two layers of fir marine plywood covered with two layers of Dynel cloth sealed with epoxy. This makes an extremely strong, watertight deck. Joel had used this system with great success on several of his more recent projects (including POPOVER) and none of those boats showed any signs of water in any joinery.

Every piece of wood in the LADY JEANNE was glued or bedded with the most modern adhesives and compounds, and screwed or bolted with bronze: not a galvanized or steel fastening anywhere!

Since the 671 General Motors Diesel had proved to be such a satisfactory engine on the Rich boat we used it again, but this time we insisted on a dry exhaust. An asbestos-wrapped Cowles muffler is installed under the deck, attached to a 6" stainless steel pipe which passes through the cockpit deck via a stainless steel deckplate and finally is braced to the wheelhouse roof. Since the engine is fresh water cooled by a Walters keel cooler there is no need for any salt water pumps or filters, and with adequate anti-freeze in the system the boat can be used year round.

Fresh water is carried in one 220 gallon aluminum tank installed under the aft cockpit with a water filter in the system to assure clear, good tasting water. This charcoal filter is inadequate protection against germs, however, so it is still important to take water from reliable sources.

Our choice of systems and appliances completely eliminated the need for a generator; this makes the engine room more spacious, life aboard quieter, and reduces our dependence on others. We did install two large storage batteries, one reserved for starting the engine, the other for lights and other appliances. One or both can be charged while the engine is running.

One of the most critical aspects in the ownership of a wooden boat is the provision of adequate ventilation at all times. In no other way can any vessel be guaranteed a long, healthy life. Wood must have a constant change of air. This presents a problem for life aboard; we are accustomed to well heated homes and want our boats to be cozy and draft-free, while still providing sufficient ventilation. On the LADY JEANNE we attacked this problem in several ways.

The main bulkhead is water tight so it blocks drafts from outside, but the forward part of the boat must still be ventilated. The cedar sealing with which the whole front half of the boat is panelled provides insulating air space, but it is left open at the top so air can circulate freely.

We also installed a 6" ventilator in the wheelhouse roof, so the air is constantly moved even when the boat is locked up tight. When we were aboard in cold weather we'd stuff a towel in this opening to prevent excessive heat loss. The use of eight opening Rostand portholes and two Bomar hatches and the four way ventilation in the wheelhouse make any combination possible for enough air at all times. In Maine we found that by opening the windshield just a little we were quite comfortable; we seldom needed anything more, though on any cruise south all openings would be needed.

Most boats have many drawers, closed closets and cupboards which we have found to be breeding places for mildew, mold and rot. For this reason most of the storage space on LADY JEANNE is open; there are only four drawers. Both hanging lockers are open; there are several shelves with high fiddles, a couple of lift-up compartments; and the storage areas under beds and dinettes are open so plastic bins or baskets may be slid in for storage of bulky items. We took aboard only those things which we used frequently, stored them neatly and visibly, and eliminated them if we found them unused.

We have lived with every possible eating arrangement on our boats and found that we enjoy raised dinettes the most. They are built into the sides of the cabin or wheelhouse, taking less floor space, but still providing a good view of the outside. Once people are seated in a dinette, they are not blocking the passages for others as often happens with dropleaf and fold-down tables. We decided to have two dinettes on this boat. The one in the wheelhouse doubles as a chart table. From its raised seat, the navigator can see as well as the skipper. The smaller one below serves as an office and an alternative for meals on hot days.

Construction was begun early in January and required exactly six months. We drove to Brooklin every Friday to check progress and make decisions, but these trips were no strain since it is only a ninety minute drive over scenic and deserted roads. How pleasant compared to the twelve hour drives required to supervise the Rich boat.

*Jeanne Merkel stands before the cedar boards which became
the hull of Joel White's LADY JEANNE.*

All the workers at the Brooklin Boat Yard: Steve, Henry, Belford, Sonny, Tim and John, took great pride in their work; to them it was not just a job but a pleasure to create something beautiful. Belford Gray was the finish carpenter most involved with the interior, and his sensitive and understanding treatment of our ideas made them a striking reality. I don't think I've ever seen a boat interior I liked more. Henry varnished the cedar, oak and fir time after time. They are warm and honey colored in contrast to the richness of the mahogany. When I was aboard I always felt as though I owned a priceless work of art: a rarity in a plastic, mass-produced world.

So often, when talking to contractors, it is a waste of breath to express ideas. Joel White not only listened but always acted on our suggestions. He was interested in the challenge of the project; he never scoffed at our ideas, no matter how novel or far-fetched. How pleasant it was to work with him.

Early on, we had a hint of the kind of boat he would build. On one of our first inspection visits he showed us the beautiful laminated oak roof carlings he had fashioned. We knew then that we had found an intelligent artist, not merely a craftsman. Later, after we expressed concern about the usual rot found in the corners of trunk cabins, he went into his own woodlot and produced fine locust corner posts with a unique design to assure water tightness. Our dream boat was in good hands.

While our weekly trips to Brooklin were the focal point of our lives while the boat was being built, the other days were filled with enjoyable outings. That winter there was very little snow and my journal records almost daily hikes, mountain explorations and ice skating.

On the first of January we climbed Parkman Mountain with Paul. The temperature was in the thirties and there was no wind. We had a wonderful, memorable day, saw a deer high on the mountain, ate lunch sprawled on a sunny ledge with a gorgeous view of lakes, islands and sea sparkling in the clear air. Lying there in the sun, Joe confided that he felt better than he had in ten years. We looked forward to a wonderful new year.

Paul continued to perform in every play produced by the Mount Desert Island High School drama department. That kept us going, picking him up after practice almost every night and often driving him to school when he missed the bus. It was a very busy winter.

With the coming of spring Joe had gone to work on POPOVER and once it was launched we went boating instead of hiking. I started work on an article about the building of this boat which I sold to WOODENBOAT magazine soon after the boat was finished. Herb Gliick, the editor of OFFSHORE magazine, read that article and called to ask if I would do three articles for him. That assignment grew into a dozen articles and was the genesis for this book. A new career for me!

Early in June we drove to Riverhead, visited many of our children, checked the nursery and did our usual maintenance work on the grounds. We brought my mother back for a cool Maine vacation.

Paul found a summer job in Bar Harbor and we settled him in a room there, close to his work. That seemed like a better solution than providing a car for a fifteen year old so he could commute. He was an independent, self-reliant young man who resisted any form of control; we agreed that "experience" would be the only teacher he would acknowledge.

"Sonny," Tim and Joel plank the hull of LADY JEANNE.

By June 21, the new LADY JEANNE was almost ready. Joe and I began daily trips to Brooklin. We would arrive each day at about 3:00 P.M. when the men were almost done for the day, and stay until midnight, cleaning and polishing. Joe crawled through every inch of the bilge, dragging the vacuum cleaner behind him. Before the boat hit the water he made sure there was not a crumb of sawdust or a wood shaving anywhere. We brought bedding, dishes, grooming and cleaning supplies aboard and spread six of my wool braided rugs on the shiny fir floors. We were ready.

Launching day dawned hot and sunny. When we got to the boatyard a crowd was already beginning to gather; boat launchings are exciting days in Maine villages where whole communities have a stake in the success of local shops. The General Motors mechanic from Billing's Marine in Stonington had already started the engine and discovered that something in the power steering had been put in backwards. The crew was racing the clock, trying to get the steering fixed in time to launch with the tide.

We had stopped in Blue Hill to buy a bottle of champagne; this time *I* would christen my namesake myself! In my haste, however, I had forgotten to bring a nylon stocking to catch the breaking glass. Belford was afraid that in smashing the bottle I would be cut, so he wrapped it with tape.

By the time the power steering was fixed there must have been a hundred people gathered; Maynard Bray from WOODENBOAT magazine was busy taking pictures. Joe climbed aboard and the ladders were taken away. My big moment was at hand!

I stood at the bow, bottle in hand, and expressed our appreciation to the wonderful men who had become our friends while building our lovely dream boat. While it is trite to compare ship launchings to childbirth, there certainly is in common a wonderful feeling of creative power. While we had not, in fact, built the beautiful craft before us, our ideas were everywhere manifest in her. We had shared in that birth and rejoiced in it.

I braced my feet on the ways and swung. The tape wrapped bottle was still intact. I swung again. Bang. Harder. BANG! This was getting silly. That bottle was so well taped that it couldn't break. Belford looked for a solution. He found a heavy crowbar and placed it against the hull. I swung with all my strength. This time the bottle crashed with a satisfying POP and I said the magic words:

"I christen you LADY JEANNE."

The crowd roared its approval and clapped as the winch whirred. LADY JEANNE slid into the clean, cold water of Center Harbor. Joe started the engine and circled around the moored boats. After a few turns he came back to the dock and I climbed aboard with the boatyard crew and their wives. How handsome Joe looked at the helm. The boat handled beautifully and everyone exclaimed over her design and layout. It was a proud and happy interlude. We returned to the dock several times until everyone who was interested had been given a ride. It was fortunate we had held off on the final coat of paint for the cockpit floor; twenty years of normal use would just about equal that day.

After everyone had a ride, we gathered in the boat shed where Aileen White, Joel's wife, had prepared food, snacks and beverages. A launching party is a casual affair where everyone who is interested in boats or involved with their construction is welcome. The wives and children of the crew, most of the staff of WOODENBOAT, other area boat builders, and even Joel's famous father, writer E. B. White, joined in the good boat talk over food and drink. It was rather like a wedding: such excitement, so many new people to meet, and too much to drink! Looking back, it is a happy blur.

During the following three weeks, the finishing touches were applied. The wall lights which were delivered late were installed, radio speaker cabinets built and positioned, and aluminum gas tanks located at Hinckley's in Manset and connected. The last coat of paint was applied to the rails and the cockpit floor.

In between, we did manage to take a few short cruises into Eggemoggin Reach to make sure all systems were operating well. On one such outing Joe smelled oil burning. We lifted the engine hatch to discover oil seeping from one side of the oil pan. Joe was furious. He had expended so much effort to have a spotless bilge and here it was awash with oil!

Back at the dock he took out his tools and found that the bolts on one whole side of the pan had not been tightened down in the factory. Evidently the paint on the engine had prevented the oil from leaking at once; it took the jarring of a few rides to crack the paint seal. Joe got out the engine manual to determine the torque pressures, and went over the whole engine pan tightening bolts. The job of cleaning the bilge took even longer and is best forgotten!

At that point we were torn between boat and family. We wanted to supervise the final work on our beautiful boat, but Michele and her young family had arrived to spend a month at a rented shore cottage in Bernard. We also wanted to spend time with them. It was back and forth between loves.

On July 18, we brought LADY JEANNE to our new 4,000 pound mooring in Southwest Harbor. We would have preferred to moor in Bass Harbor but it was crowded with lobster boats; the harbor master could find no room for us. First, we put the mooring near a ledge in the inner harbor, but the resident seagulls gave us no peace. We soon had the mooring moved to the very center of the harbor entrance, across from the Coast Guard Station.

The remainder of the summer was a blur of visits; the beds in our little house never got a chance to cool off between occupants. After Michele and her family went back to Pittsburgh there was a constant stream: Marie, Paul, Jeff, Jeanne and Chris with Beth and Shoshana, my brother John and his family, and my sister Audrey with her husband George. During all of this Joe and I lived on the boat. The house was full. I planned and cooked dinners, changed beds and planned outings.

We took everyone on what we came to think of as the visitor cruise: up Somes Sound, into Northeast Harbor, out to Bunker Ledge to see the seals on the rocks and, if weather and time permitted, around Baker and Great Cranberry Islands.

The boat was much admired by all, as was the beautiful island we now call home. In between visits, however, we had an assortment of bugs to get out of the boat. We began by running the batteries down by using the refrigeration units without adequate running time. I began the practice of bringing ice frozen in Tupperware bread boxes to limit use of the batteries.

Then came a problem with the hydraulic steering: the pulley was the wrong size so the steering didn't work when the engine was run at less than 800 rpm, and that was too fast for safe docking. A new pulley solved that. The next problem was a leak in the same steering unit. We struggled with it for a couple of weeks before we realized that the pump was cracked. We drove to Rockland for a replacement and Joe cleaned the bilge AGAIN! Even new boats need a resident mechanic.

When the final bills for the boat arrived we had stern reality to face, Though we had saved most of the proceeds from the sale of the Rich boat, arranged a new bank loan, sold our Ferry Road house and POPOVER we were still short. To get the final payment we had to remortgage one of our nursery buildings, giving up our 7½% mortgage to refinance at 13%. What a blow! We were in debt over our heads again.

By September we had everything under control and all the company had gone. Joe and I set out for a few days alone. We moored near Black Island where we had salvaged our hen house lumber. Then we cruised to Burnt Coat Harbor on Swans Island, where we picked enough raspberries for a pot of jam. After a few days we hopped over to Eggemoggin Reach. The boat was wonderfully comfortable. This was the life we had been dreaming of for so long.

Later in September Marie and her husband Pete arrived for a visit, and in October Jeff came back bringing his wife Mary for a few days. Between boat outings, mountain climbing, berry picking and visits the fall passed all too quickly.

Near the end of October a violent storm raged along the coast tearing many boats from their moorings. Joe and I just made it to the LADY JEANNE before the storm, and tried to ride it out on the mooring, but the Manset shore was fearfully exposed. We finally started the engine and beat our way down Somes Sound to the safety of a mooring off Cochran's Boat Yard. We would store the boat there for the winter.

Once the boat was safe inside we made two trips to New York in quick succession. One in November was to close the new mortgage and another at Christmas. We visited all of our children in their homes and then had a huge Christmas feast for everyone at the nursery. There we met Elaine's husband, Rich Tomao, for the first time. They had been married in a private ceremony that September and only notified us after the fact.

We put in long hours doing our usual work at the nursery, and by the time we left for Maine Joe was sick with what turned out to be a miserable flu. A few days later I came down with it. Paul escaped, which was fortunate, since he was due to perform in several presentations of FIDDLER ON THE ROOF. What a year this had been. Even retired, we had been just as busy as ever. And, it was not over yet.

At 6:00 A.M. on the last day of December the phone rang. It was our nursery manager, Fran Burding, with bad news. During the night a drug crazed young man had broken into the smaller of our nursery buildings and started a fire which completely destroyed the beautiful apartment on the second floor. Originally, that floor had been finished as a conference room and office, but when we moved to Maine we had contracted the few alterations necessary to make a rental unit. We had been just about ready to look for a tenant.

That night we lost the income we had been counting on to pay our rent in Maine. We would have to tighten our belts still further. We had a grim New Year's Day. Even our hens had stopped laying.

1981

Fortunately, the enrollment at the nursery is normally lower during January and February, so the children from the burned building could be cared for in our two other buildings while repairs were made. We had to be thankful that the fire had not gone through the roof. Though the apartment was a total loss, the insurance would cover new ceilings and the restoration for the nursery rooms on the first floor. There was less money to live on than planned, but life went on.

We went skiing on the carriage roads of Mount Desert Island and hiked the trails as soon as the snow melted. In February we visited Michele in Pittsburgh and in April we went to New York for a week of scrubbing and weeding at the nursery. It was a terrible shock to walk into the ruins of our once lovely apartment.

Back in Maine it was soon time to launch LADY JEANNE. Though she was brand new, Joe had ordered a full paint job. (That was before the fire.) The estimate had been $2,500. When the bill came for painting and winter storage, plus a couple of very small projects, the total was $6,271. Soon after, the property tax assessment for the boat arrived: $900. The insurance bill, due in July, was $890, even with a $5,000 deductible. The handwriting was on the wall. It would only be a matter of time before we would have to decide: back to work or sell the boat!

Once again, Paul moved to Bar Harbor to work in a restaurant during the summer. Joe and I lived aboard and cruised around the local islands and harbors. Unbelievably, five of our children were expecting babies between May and August. We tried to keep in touch with all of them, so we didn't venture far from our phone. Besides, there was no money for the extra fuel and the unexpected expenses of vacation cruising.

On May 24, Genia Nicole was born to Joe and Nancy, then on June 9, tiny Rivkah joined Jeanne's family. (On that same day Joe and I went sadly to Bobby Rich's funeral.) After Renee's baby, Jessica, arrived on June 27, Joe and I cut out for a mini-vacation, since the next baby was not due until August.

We got only as far as Swans Island, where we had two lovely sunny days hiking and picking berries. We were about to leave for Boothbay Harbor when fog rolled in. The island was socked in for five days. When it finally cleared, the steam had gone out of us. Joe was nervous and tense. We went back home to check on all the mothers and then planned to try again, but another surprise awaited us.

Joe's brother Ed had not visited us in years but he was just divorced and between jobs. He called to see if he could spend a few weeks with us in Maine. Joe and Ed had been very good friends as children and Joe was delighted at the prospect of a visit with his brother.

Ed dropped from the skies in mid-July, flying the beautiful bi-wing stunt plane he had built himself. As engineer, jet and stunt pilot, Ed was full of life. He put on exhibition shows over the harbor and made a host of friends. He took everyone for airplane rides. After a few boat rides around the islands he insisted that he wanted to climb every mountain (I guess the boat rides were too tame for him). The boat was abandoned while we packed picnic lunches and hiked.

Soon, Ed became involved having fun with new friends, so Joe and I decided to finish the cruise we had started earlier. On the last day of July we started out early in the morning and reached Boothbay Harbor by five in the afternoon. It had been three years since we had laid over on a mooring off Brown's Wharf.

We visited Robinhood again and picked raspberries once more on Little Knubble. Returning to Boothbay, we found a mooring at the yacht club where we treated ourselves to lunch on a rainy day. We hiked to Southport Island and then back to Boothbay, several times, to spend long evenings at the Tugboat listening to their good musicians. On the way home we laid over in Friendship where we walked to Hatchet Cove and saw the new Lash-built boat, SKIPPER.

We got back to Bass Harbor just in time; on August 8, Michele called to report the safe delivery of Anna. Then Ed's son Jack (born the same day as our Paul) arrived by air for a few days of mountain climbing with us before they left in Ed's plane on August 13. On the 24th Jeff proudly proclaimed the arrival of his first child, Jennifer. That made five new granddaughters in the family. What a summer!

By the time September rolled around it was obvious that Joe was not well. All through the summer he had been getting more and more anxious. While we had so many children to worry about, the boat to take care of, and company in the house, he tried to hold himself together, but by mid-September he was almost non-functional, crying again, lying on the couch, unable to accomplish anything. He had not been under medical care since we moved to Maine, but it was obvious that his depression had returned. Just as bad as the first time. I called my brother John to seek advice.

Since Joe is a World War II veteran, John advised us to seek care at the Veteran's Hospital in Augusta where John worked. I took Joe there on September 17. The doctor said that Joe was too depressed to chance out-patient care. He would have to stay in the hospital for a couple of weeks, at least until they worked out a successful treatment program.

I stayed with John and Beppie in Readfield for a couple of days while Joe got settled in the hospital, and then drove home alone.

Eric Edwards of Southwest Boat Corporation had agreed to keep an eye on the boat in our absence, but I was anxious to check. Hoping to have a few more days on the water in October, we had left the boat on her mooring in Manset, but it looked like our 1981 cruising season was over. Fearing the gusty, late September winds, Joe had instructed me to stay ashore while he was in the hospital.

Driving past Southwest Harbor I couldn't help but note the calm sea with LADY JEANNE gently swinging on her mooring. Love, honor and cherish are easy, but the heck with OBEY! I went on to Bass Harbor, fed the cat and hens, picked some vegetables and gathered eggs. Then I threw oars and some food in the car, and made a beeline for Manset.

Rowing out to LADY JEANNE felt so good after the long car ride and the tension of the last few weeks. I determined to spend the night aboard. It would be only the second time alone. The seagulls had left their calling cards, purple berries and tiny shells which took forever to clean up. I realized, once again, how lucky I was to have a captain who could keep my namesake in yacht condition.

Chores done and darkness creeping in, I lit the Dickinson oil stove, made myself a ladylike supper of toast with cream cheese, a salad and tea, read a bit, and climbed into bed by nine-thirty. In spite of my worries about Joe, the gentle motion worked its usual magic. I was soon asleep.

I had shut down the stove before sleeping so when I woke the boat was quite cold. No, very cold! I snuggled deeper and dozed, waiting for the sun. It always rises, but sometimes, obscured by clouds or fog, it doesn't give much heat. I was lucky, the next time I opened my eyes a bright, sunny morning greeted me. To compensate for my skimpy supper I treated myself to an oversized breakfast that included two poached eggs and the wonderful raspberry jam I'd made when we were stuck in the fog on Swans Island.

I wiped down the boat, careful to do a good job. I would not let Joe down; the boat would get good care in his absence. Then I worked on an article for OFFSHORE. In spite of illness and family responsibilities, my deadline loomed.

By 2:00 P.M. the wind had picked up considerably. The Coast Guard weather station advised that we were in for three days of nasty wind and rain. If I was going to make the long row to the Manset dock, I'd better get started. With the wind strong from the south I'd be blown into the harbor and not out to sea, but I didn't relish the ignominy of landing on private property. I closed the boat up tight. The big roof ventilator would keep the air moving. Everything seemed to be in order, but the mooring line did look shorter than usual.

"Probably wound around the chain again," I thought. "I wish Doug (our mooring man) would get around to that new rope we had ordered ... should I call him?" I decided not to bother him. Eric had promised to bring the boat to the dock by Friday. It had been all right all summer. Surely it would be good for three more days.

I climbed in the dinghy with care in the increasing chop. I'm no great swimmer, and the late September water is already cold enough to finish off a careless yachtsman in minutes. I rowed mightily for the Manset dock, bitterly bemoaning the poor design of our dinghy with its inboard oarlocks which were forever slipping the oars just when they were needed most.

"One of these days," I promised myself, "we will get a real Maine peapod for our tender." Narrowly avoiding grounding off Bob Hinckley's shore, I finally reached the town dock.

Home. Feed the animals. Freeze more vegetables. It is amazing how much food a 16'x20' garden produces in Maine. Supper, a bath and to bed. Lonely, lonely.

I awakened to a dreary, windy and rainy morning. I washed my hair and then typed two long letters to children. Twelve-thirty. The post office was closed. I gathered the eggs, made a shopping list and collected library books. One-fifteen. I cranked up the old VW and went off to post my letters, visit the library and shop for food. On the way back, I took a turn along the Manset shore to check the boat.

As I rounded the corner a great emptiness greeted by eyes. Checking the rear view mirror first, I pulled over to the side of the road. No, my eyes had not deceived me. The LADY JEANNE was GONE! The red mooring ball was still bouncing gaily in the stiff breeze, one red flag snapped on the flagpole at the Coast Guard Base across the harbor, but the boat was nowhere in sight.

"Oh, no! Oh, no!" I gasped. "Oh, poor Joe, his beautiful boat, my beautiful boat, Oh, God!"

Then, a calming thought. Perhaps Eric had made room at the dock and, seeing the ugly weather coming, had decided to bring the boat in early. But surely he would have called. I was home all morning.

"Keep calm, keep calm, back up the car. Turn around." Back to Southwest Harbor. Down Clark Point Road. Park the car. Walk ... RUN ... down to the dock at Southwest Boat. NOT THERE ... not yet ... "WALK all the way to the end, don't fall, the tide is so low. NO, the boat is not here ..."

I looked up and down the harbor. There were hundreds of boats, but no LADY JEANNE!

Running then, tears coming ... no way to stop them. Into Eric's office. "Eric, did you move the boat? It's GONE!"

"Take it easy, Jeanne. No. No, I didn't. Stay right here. Sit down!"

Eric pulled on his slicker and boots, then left on the run. I collapsed into a chair, weeping bitterly.

"Oh, Joe, poor Joe, your beautiful boat ... and I was going to take such good care of it. And we only have half enough insurance with a $5,000 deductible and no savings. Oh, it's not fair. All the worry, and now this!"

Sternly I scolded myself: "No one is hurt. It could be worse. Calm down. Blow your nose. Time enough for tears when you know the worst."

Eric rushed back into the office and picked up the phone. He dialed the familiar number of the Coast Guard Station.

"Do you have any info on a LADY JEANNE? ... great boat, looks like a lobster boat ... green ... seems to have broken loose from her mooring? ... right across from you in Manset. Okay, thanks."

Eric put down the phone.

"It's drifting on the Manset shore, around the point!" He raced for the door. I was at his heels. "Wait here, Jeanne!" he said, but I shook my head. I had to know.

In Eric's car we sped up Clark Point Road to the head of the harbor. Eric spotted the LADY JEANNE drifting shoreward. Rocks! Wind and waves seemed more violent.

"We're going the wrong way!" Eric snapped, turning the car roughly back to Southwest Boat. Eric jumped out and ran ahead calling for John. Together, they leapt down to the dock. The engine of Eric's runabout sprang to life.

Across the harbor, spray flying, they raced. A Coast Guard boat was hovering in the area, just watching it seemed, while our life's savings went aground on the rocks.

"Why can't they put a line on her?" I thought. I saw Doug Beal in his workboat plowing toward the LADY JEANNE from the inner harbor. Help was at hand, if only they weren't too late!

I stood on the dock, tears streaming down my face in the rain. I could see the LADY JEANNE aground on the far shore. She was just barely visible behind the schooner KATHLEEN which was moored in mid-harbor. Eric in his yellow slicker ... he's on the bow ... the wheelhouse door opened ... moments later a puff of smoke from the dry exhaust. Minutes seemed like hours. A lady in a red windbreaker put her arm around my shoulders.

"I think they'll get her off."

A young lad from the boat yard thought not: "The tide's still going out. They'll probably have to wait till the tide turns to get her free."

I couldn't watch any longer. Back into Eric's office. Blow my nose. Walk toward the Coast Guard Station, then back to the dock. Afraid to look, I walked back out on the long pier. No LADY JEANNE on the shore. At last, I spotted her moving slowly toward me. John pulled in with the runabout.

"Eric's bringing her in. I don't think she's leaking. We'll tie her up to the yard's workboat over there."

I ran across the plank between the floats and stood at the stern of the workboat, ready to take a line. John docked the runabout and went to the bow. Moving slowly, Eric drew alongside at the helm of the LADY JEANNE. It was too good to be true. She seemed unhurt. We made her fast and I hugged Eric and thanked John, my heart overflowing.

We opened the engine hatches and pumped the bilge, waited, and pumped again. I unscrewed the forward floor hatches and we looked for damage. There was nothing to see. Clean bilges. No water coming in!

"There may be a bit of paint scraped off the bottom, but that's no problem." Eric assured me. He had cut his hand in his haste and his Englishman's red blood was everywhere, but the boat was unharmed. Fortunately, she had grounded on a section of gravel beach instead of on the menacing rocks. Pure luck.

Marveling once more at her beauty, for the hundredth time I thought: "Joel White, you built us some fine boat!"

John made fast the spring lines. I started wiping up the wet footsteps, the traces of blood and the raindrops that had blown through the open doors. Doug came to see if there was anything he could do, bitterly remorseful over the communication failure. He'd thought we were going to move the mooring to Bass Harbor and had planned to do both jobs, new line and move the mooring, at one time. He promised to inspect the mooring, discover what had failed, and get a new line on right away.

The wind was still strong when Eric checked the lines on all the boats in his care before going home at four-thirty. The boat yard was deserted. I drove to Bass Harbor, put the wet, lonely cat in the basement, ate a very late lunch, had a quick bath, and then returned to the LADY JEANNE.

"I'll sleep aboard tonight," I thought, "I'd better check the bilge pump once in a while, just in case."

Joe would be home soon, feeling better, I hoped. Our children and grandchildren were all well. The boat was safe. The rain drummed on the roof, the lightning flashed and the thunder boomed, but I was cozy, my kettle whistling. I made some tea and a sandwich, then lit a candle and watched the light play on the varnished wood while I snuggled into my warm bunk and thought: "Only a few more nights alone."

"Next time a mooring line looks short, I'll surely double up, somehow, no matter how choppy it is. I've been spared this time, but I should start to learn."

"Never again will I pull that exasperated, inpatient tone when Joe announces that he's off to check the boat once more before bedtime. I'll bundle up and go with him. Two heads are always better than one. You just can't check a boat too often ... in Maine in September ... in Connecticut in May. Anytime."

Eric hauled the boat soon after and put it inside one of his big sheds. He agreed to let Joe work on her, himself. The only question was, would Joe ever be well enough again to tackle that big job.

It took two miserable months before Joe's condition stabilized. He had to return to the hospital twice before they found a combination of drugs to fight his anxiety and depression without unacceptable side effects. It was a lonely, tortured time for me, too. I wondered if life would ever be normal again. At last, Joe began to feel better.

I was desperate to see all the new grandchildren, so we arranged a family reunion at the nursery on the day after Thanksgiving. Paul and I took turns with much of the driving so the trip wouldn't be too stressful for Joe. We spent a day with my mother in Sea Cliff, then had a lovely Thanksgiving dinner with my sister Audrey and her family in Cold Spring Harbor.

The next day all nine children gathered at the nursery with eight spouses, seven toddlers between two and five, and the five new baby girls! What a day. There will never be another like it! Photo-opportunities all day long.

That evening we went to Brasby's Restaurant for a grown-ups only dinner. We had hired three baby sitters for all the grandchildren. When nineteen adults sit around a table, you need a LONG table! Looking at our family, we wondered how we had ever managed.

1982

During the winter Joe continued to improve. We took long hikes almost every day and went cross-country skiing a total of forty-one times. We were thankful that we lived in such a beautiful place; there were so many trails and carriage roads to hike and ski. We had long talks, trying to decide how we could best survive. We had to face the realization that our dream of living aboard year round in our lovely little ship would not work. That life no longer seemed possible.

We had hoped to cruise south in the winters, but reports of spiraling marina charges, overcrowding on the inland waterway, and the dangers posed by drug traffickers made us reject that dream. Though we had built a year-round boat, the water in Maine was too rough and cold in the winter; rowing out to our moored boat was often dangerous and uncomfortable. The cost of dockage, even in Maine, had risen with the cost of shorefront land. Both had escalated beyond our reach. Maintaining a rental house, we were pouring money away with no security in sight. Joe had twice succumbed to terrifying depression; we could not depend on his continued health and strength. Finally, managing the nursery from a distance of five hundred miles was proving to be an impossible task. It was time for a new game plan.

We decided to put both the day care business and the boat on the market. If we could sell either of them we would have enough cash to build a small cabin in Maine, so we would not continue to waste money on rent. Once the nursery was sold we would have an income to support us until we were eligible for social security.

Though Joe had been completely disabled for years by his depression, we had never applied for disability income. Our small income from the nursery was just not adequate; each month we were falling further behind. Joe was not really well enough to work and, if I went to work, he would be alone and lonely. No possession was worth the sacrifice of the hours of our lives. We had worked too hard and too long. Now we needed time. Time together. With our own land we might yet find a way to own a boat, if we could bring it home and do our own work.

Our hikes became more purposeful as we walked the boundaries of every parcel of available land. Shorefront was out of the question, but it might still be possible to find an inland parcel we could afford.

In May, Joe started working on the boat. Beginning at the top, he hand-sanded each section, removed all dust with vacuum cleaner and tack-rag, then carefully painted. Everyone commented on the beautiful job he did. He might have been very sick, but he had not lost his touch!

Mothers' Day and my birthday were celebrated in New York with many of our children, and our 34th wedding anniversary in Southwest Harbor at the Happy Crab Restaurant with my brother John and his family. In June, Paul was graduated from high school; another milestone for us. Our last child was ready to leave the nest. He was soon settled in Bar Harbor, working at George's Restaurant, and managing his own life.

We saw him for an evening once in a while but accepted his independence. Though you never stop worrying about your children, day to day responsibility for them ceases once they are out of high school. If he stayed out late we didn't know about it, so we didn't worry. We had learned that being tired for the next day's work is the best cure for intemperance, and that earning enough money for food and rent leaves little for debauchery. We had done our best; now it was up to him.

Toward the end of June the LADY JEANNE was launched by an enormous crane from the dock at Southwest Boat. It was terrifying, watching our treasure swinging high above. We resolved to find a yard with a travel-lift or ways for the next winter. Joe's fine paint job should last two years and perhaps by then the boat would be sold. In the meantime, we would enjoy it.

We had Doug Beal move our mooring closer to the Manset shore, so we wouldn't have such a long, dangerous row. Our harbor couldn't have been more pleasant, surrounded as it was by the mountains of Mount Desert, the entrance to Somes Sound, and several spruce-crowned protecting islands.

Early in the day we would sun ourselves, then while Joe kept the boat spotless I would read or write. After lunch we would take a short cruise or else row ashore to shop, pick berries, look at land, or hike.

Every evening as the sun set behind Western Mountain several families would enjoy evening outings in small sailboats, while the Hinckley charter fleet came and went just to the east of us. Often, the schooners from Camden would sail dramatically into the harbor. Amid cheerful bustle J. E. RIGGIN, ADVENTURE, TIMBERWIND or MERCANTILE would drop sail and anchor between us and the Coast Guard Station. Far down the harbor the crew on MISS EMILY would shuck the day's scallops and, by the sound of things, be polishing off a few brews to ease the pain.

Joe and I would savor our evening's ration of wine and cheese while enjoying the show. As darkness descended I would fix our light supper; we'd linger over coffee in our glass-enclosed wheelhouse, letting our eyes grow accustomed to the dark, waiting for the moon, counting the stars.

In August we found a four acre parcel in Bernard. It was just the kind of land I had dreamed of: blueberry ledge and hundreds of cedar, spruce, pine and larch trees on land that had been burned over about fifty years before. The trees were still young. Though a cedar bog stretched across the front, there was a high and dry, south-facing building site. While four ravens were in possession (and still are), Barbara Sawyer held title. I used my credit card to put a deposit on the property and arranged a loan. We would pay it off when we sold something, and in the meantime we could get the site cleared and bring in a driveway.

I had been feeling quite depressed myself: change of life blues, plus worries about Joe's health, and money, but having the land cheered me up. My own trees, at last. When I finally got a cabin on this beautiful land I vowed never to move again!

One afternoon, old neighbors from Bayville who were just about our ages, Bob and Eva Claus, turned up at our Bass Harbor house. We had not seen them since we moved to Jamesport in 1961. They had been good friends and we had lots of catching up to do. Bob had been suffering from stomach problems and was recuperating from an operation. The next Christmas card reported his death. He never got a chance to enjoy his well-earned retirement. We hoped that would not happen to us.

During the summer our short cruises took us to all the beautiful surrounding harbors where we often spent a couple of days enjoying a different view. When we could find a mooring we took long walks; if anchored, we stayed close to LADY JEANNE.

One weekend on Swans Island we had an enjoyable candle-lit dinner at the new Bridge Restaurant, and the next morning we walked to the Oddfellows Hall where a community breakfast was being served. It was just delicious. It was raining, but someone gave us a ride back to the boat. I enjoy cooking, but it is fun to eat out once in a while.

During the fall our cruising was interspersed with work on the land. Every sunny day we went boating; every overcast or rainy day we cut down and pruned trees. Once the lower branches were removed from all the trees in an area, Joe took the lawnmower to the brush: overgrown blueberries, rhodora and sheep laurel. I planted two apple trees and transplanted the strawberry and raspberry bushes I'd been raising to our own land.

We went to every Baked Bean and Casserole Supper at two churches and the fire house. I hiked every Tuesday with the Footloose Friends, an offshoot of the Friends of the Library and I became involved with a book discussion program and with efforts to expand the library. We made many new friends so this little community became "home" in more ways than we had ever experienced before. While we had been so busy working and raising our big family we had not had time to participate in the life of our villages.

It was soon time to find a winter shelter for LADY JEANNE. We didn't want to insult her with another crane hauling and launching, so I started calling boatyards. Most of them would only store inside those boats which were in need of lots of yard-supplied labor (i.e. big yard bills). We only wanted storage. I finally lined up a space in Billing's shed at Stonington, but cancelled that reservation when Jock Williams found room for the boat in his shed. He would take us without a big work order.

With the boat inside, we were ready to go to New York for a long Thanksgiving visit. Once again, we visited my mother and most of our children in their homes, then worked late every night at the nursery.

We had put out the word that we were looking for a buyer, and had three people waiting to be interviewed. After talking to all of them we selected the youngest couple as the most appropriate purchasers. They were about the ages we had been when we started the business, and they seemed to have lots of energy and enthusiasm. We agreed on a price and terms, (as well as taking back the mortgage for them,) and arranged for the writing of contracts.

While we would have preferred to turn over the business on the first of the year (less income tax work for us,) but found the legal work took too long. It was the first of February before the new owners could take over. In the interim we went back to Maine for nineteen days, then returned to Riverhead to move our personal possessions out of the nursery. As Jeanne and her family were still living in the apartment in the main building, which the new owners wanted, we helped them move to another apartment.

During that holiday season we saw every family member except Jeff. Our schedule had us hopping: Boston, Riverhead ... Sea Cliff ... Pittsburgh ... then back to Riverhead and Boston. By the time we drove into our Bass Harbor driveway early on New Year's Eve, we were worn out. We took our baths, had a quiet supper and went to bed. These long, complicated trips could not have been managed without the help of dear friends, Jeanie and George Gilpin and Pam Bergeron. During our absences they watered almost fifty plants, cared for our nine hens, and visited our lonely kitty, Zonk.

Without the nursery to worry about, we expected the next years to be easier. It had been difficult to operate such a personal business from a distance of five hundred miles. Joe kept singing his favorite song: "Our Day Will Come." I kept drawing house plans. That's almost as much fun as designing boats.

1983

During the winter we had talked with several contractors and decided that a small log cabin would be the most appropriate, low-maintenance solution for our retirement home. With the down-payment from the nursery sale we could pay all our bills and buy a Ward Log Home Package. A mortgage would still be needed, but that would be paid off while the nursery was being paid off. We would have our home free and clear when I reached sixty-eight years of age.

We installed a big culvert where the driveway would be brought in, grubbed out all the roots, sphagnum moss and topsoil, and had several loads of sand and gravel spread. With the addition of another culvert, we could get across the bog. Soon we were able to drive into our land.

On every trip to New York we had returned with a piece of furniture. Since our little rental house was a furnished one, it had become totally overcrowded as we accumulated the possessions of our lifetimes. Every chair, table and chest had seen better days, having survived the hobbies and growing pains of our big family. I set to work refinishing and recovering. Every piece held memories; I had no desire for new things. As I catalogued and packed my books I dreamed of the new house which would have enough shelves to hold them, at last.

In April, the septic system was installed and the well drilled. It delivered ten gallons per minute at one-hundred and seventy feet. In May, we helped unload the big trailer which brought our log home kit; it was stored in Elwin Hodgdon's barn. After Jason the Mason built our footings and a poured foundation Elwin started work on the building.

Every morning Joe would head for the boat to get it ready for the summer, and I would join the crew building our house. Elwin, Shirley Cummings, Ben Hodgdon and Tim (Elwin's nephew and son-in-law) were unfailingly kind and patient with me. They found tasks I could do and didn't make any macho remarks (at least that I could hear) about having a woman on the job. Building the house was a dream come true for me. Since log homes come pre-cut, the assembly only took four weeks.

By mid-June the pine panelling on the interior was complete and the decks begun. I set to work sanding and varnishing. Once the boat was ready Joe joined me, and we did the whole inside with Captain's varnish. It will never have to be done again. The cedar logs were left natural, only sanding and washing off of stains were necessary; they will age to a soft gray.

It took two weeks of aggravation to get a power pole permit and then four charges of dynamite to get the pole into the ledge, but at last we had lights. With a power sander, work on the inside progressed faster.

The boat was moved outside so Joe could paint the bottom. Only a few days later a lightning storm destroyed the shed in which it had been stored. Lady Luck watched over LADY JEANNE that year: that was her second narrow escape. The Billing's shed we had originally planned to store in had also been lost to a dreadful fire during the winter.

We launched early in July and moved to our Manset mooring but the whole summer whizzed by with only a few short cruises, though we lived aboard from launch to haul. At least, we could enjoy mornings and evenings on the water, but both of us worked on the house all day. We were determined to be in before winter.

Our daughter Marie, convinced at last that her troubled marriage was unsalvageable, came to spend the summer in our rented house. She and Paul visited us on the boat, where they made sumptuous late breakfasts and we all talked endlessly.

Joe at the helm of LADY JEANNE

The rugs were laid in our dream cottage on the third of October and we moved in three days later. Our one bedroom cabin proved to be wonderfully cozy, facing south and overlooking our beautiful trees, berry ledge and Western Mountain. It is heated with a Resolute wood stove and three portable electric heaters which take off the chill on days too warm for a wood fire. Except for the bathroom, pantry and bedroom, the house is all open, so it is spacious and easy to heat. One end of the living area is my study with a big file desk and all my books. As we had watched our own parents get older we'd realized the dangers and difficulties of bathtubs, so we installed a stall shower. The laundry is conveniently located in the bathroom, there are no stairs to fall down, and all the windows are in reach. Now we can get old. No nursing homes for us!

Yacht broker Jarvis Newman had our boat advertised in several magazines and had showed several prospects but, while all agreed that LADY JEANNE was beautiful, no one was willing to come close to our asking price. We knew what it would cost to replace her and we were unwilling to take a loss. Fall came, and we hauled again at Jock Williams' Hall Quarry yard.

Eventually the house cost more than anticipated (they always do) and we were still carrying two other hefty mortgages: the big nursery building and the boat. At that point, we agreed: we were tired of being in debt. Owning a beautiful boat was not worth the price we were paying. Now we would give anything for peace of mind, so the asking price was reduced.

1984

After a winter of hiking, skiing, and learning to live with a wood stove, spring returned. Camden yacht broker Bill Page began to send us fussy boat seekers. One of them gave us a deposit and then changed his mind. Another loved the boat so much that he bought a set of plans from Joel; it turned out that he owned a boat shop and could get his own men to build a boat for him. (I'd be willing to bet it could not hold a candle to the one Joel built for us.)

Tax time rolled around and we had no money saved to pay state and federal income taxes. The local boat tax was due again, too, and we still hadn't paid the last year's bill. We were getting desperate.

Bill was advised to drop the price again. This time he came up with a serious buyer. Stan Griskivich had read my article in WOODENBOAT about the building of the LADY JEANNE; he had vowed that someday he'd buy her but, the earlier asking price had been out of his reach. He made us an offer. We gulped, and agreed, thankful that at least our treasure would belong to someone who loved her.

We paid off our boat mortgage and all our overdue bills, bought a 1980 economy car to replace the rusted-out Comet, and put what was left in the bank. Sadly, it was not much to show for a lifetime of hard work. How fortunate that we had started our own business all those years before. At least, we had the equity in two commercial buildings on a busy street in a county center, and the income from the sale of our business. We had worked incredibly hard, but for ourselves ... we were still self-supporting, no burden on our children, or on society.

If Joe had not been sick, IF we had not lost part of our income in the fire, IF we had been able and willing to go back to work, IF we had not spent money foolishly so often, IF, IF we could have kept our dream boat. We turned firmly away from what might have been.

We had enjoyed absolutely priceless years of boating with our children. Three times we had designed our dream boat and watched those dreams become reality; six times we had lovingly restored and proudly used previously owned boats. As the time came we watched each of these go out of our lives, turned the corner, and looked ahead.

With unforgettable anticipation we had awaited the arrival of each of our children; knowing them and sharing their lives has been our privilege. We have watched our "living arrows" leave our nest not with sadness, but with pride at their competence and hope their love of life would be equal to every situation.

Our dreams ... of beautiful children and of beautiful boats ... now are memories. If experience is the best teacher, we should have learned a few things by now about boats and kids. We still make some new mistake every day, but that is what living is all about. In the remaining chapters I will share some conclusions I have drawn from these thirty years.

10

CRUISING WITH KIDS

Joe takes the kids for a row near Fort Ticonderoga. 1955.
Joey, Joe, Renee, Jeff and Michele.

When I told Joey I was planning to publish this book, his response was that I should try for a more humorous slant: something on the order of Erma Bombeck. Well, Joey, I enjoy Erma's zany perspective, but mine is different. There is no way I could or should talk about children or see life through her eyes. I think there is room in the world for both of us.

Erma humorously describes a losing battle against dirt, laziness, incompetence and changing values. I have tried to *win* that battle. Reading extensively, I have tried to garner the insights of thoughtful minds. Taking my mother's early example, I have relished each day's projects. I have never thought of WORK as a dirty, four-letter word. It might be square, but I hardly think of anything as work. Everything I do is FUN. The only problem is that there are not enough hours in the day, and my legs and feet are starting to give out.

I suppose our kids have done as many cute or comical things as any children; they have also gotten in and out of as many scrapes, and existed in rooms that could only be cleaned with a hoe and shovel. In this story I have not violated their confidences or betrayed their secrets. Some of them would like to write, and one day they may tell their own stories. I will not steal their thunder. Seen from their perspective, it will be completely different.

I wanted to have a big family, so all my children really were "wanted children," with all that implies. During all the years of parenting I have tried to learn HOW to parent, learn from my mistakes. As I look back now, I know that this on the job training is all that any parents have and, today most only have a couple of children. By the time they learn, their opportunity to profit from their experience is already over. If only I knew in 1949 what I know now, I might have been a more effective parent.

In a word, that is my "slant." If I can share what I've learned, my life will have more meaning and purpose. I will not have wasted all that experience.

No, Joey, I'm no Erma Bombeck. Just your Mom.

If you've tried boating with kids you know its pitfalls; if you have been lucky, you know its pleasures. If you've never tried, you need to know what's involved before taking the plunge. Bringing young children cruising is serious business. All the parents I've known have placed their children at the top of their life lists of treasures, but almost everyone is lazy or irresponsible on occasion. None of us ever wants to endanger a child, yet every boating season is marred with tragedy. One summer weekend we watched the ingredients being assembled for just such a disaster.

We were anchored in the sheltered harbor of an off-shore Maine island and had been fogbound for three days. It was early evening on the third of July and, realizing that the small general store would be closed for the holiday, we had rowed in and walked up for extra groceries. Laden with supplies we returned to the float to find our dinghy was missing. A quick survey of the harbor revealed it proceeding dockward tied to the stern of a small boat. The skipper had obviously borrowed it to get out to his own boat, a common occurrence which is not considered reprehensible here in Maine. No one would refuse to lend a boat for such a purpose.

We waited on the crowded dock while he tied up, retrieved our property, then watched in stunned disbelief while a total of nineteen persons boarded that twenty foot boat. From the conversations we overheard, all were bound for their camps on an island in Blue Hill Bay. The passengers included three young mothers with infants in arms, three young men, an older couple, a couple of teenagers, a gaggle of toddlers and a grizzled grandfather.

Cases of beer and hard liquor, boxes of Pampers, worn sleeping bags, and duffle bags of clothes and blankets crowded the cockpit. There was not an inch of space to spare once all had climbed aboard. I'm morally certain there was not a good life jacket for every person aboard. Life jackets on old Maine boats tend to be rotten, anyway.

They left the dock without a dinghy and soon disappeared into the fog, by then absolutely impenetrable. I don't know what kind of internal guidance that skipper relied on, but I truly feared that they would never reach their destination. I suppose they did, somehow, for the local news broadcasts would have been full of the tragedy if they had connected with any of the countless reefs on their route.

Rain and fog continued through the whole weekend, and my thoughts returned time and again to that fun-bound group. Were the children cared for? Did the Pampers run out? Did the grownups get drunk and fight when the going got rough? I've thought about them all many times in the years since, wondering how they could have exposed themselves and their children to such danger! The first requirement for cruising with young children is: mature, responsible parents.

Owning a boat involves you in considerable work, expense and time, and tests your character as nothing else can. Before making that investment in a cruising boat, be sure your family has sampled the water. Moving from a 16' daysailer or a 19' center console fisherman can be a major social change for a family accustomed to a boat being Dad's toy (or Mom's and Dad's). To me, boating is wonderful, BUT some people get seasick. Some little ones are terrified when a sailboat heels. Others panic with the first roar of a noisy engine and still others may refuse to wear a life jacket. While there are pills for seasickness and children do adjust to heeling, noise, and the necessity of safety gear, you should avoid the initial disappointment that must result if you surprise the family with a boat they reject.

We were lucky: when we went for our first cruise with Joe's friend, George, our first four kids were all under four years of age, but they accepted the whole experience joyfully. Getting such little tots to behave on a boat seems like an impossible task, but Joe and I already had the children organized before we discovered boats. When my father's untimely death had forced my mother out to work, I had helped raise my five younger siblings. That was hard-won but invaluable experience.

By the time I had four of my own children, I had learned to negotiate firm contracts with them. I have found this management tool indispensable to parenting, and especially to boating with kids. The basis of these contracts is the child's understanding and acceptance of the fact that when a parent speaks he <u>must</u> listen and obey. Long before you board ship you have to persuade your children that you mean what you say. If, when you call your toddler he thinks it's a great game to run in the opposite direction, you have some work to do if you don't want that little man or lady overboard!

A program of obedience training is NOT punishment, though in our society dogs are better treated in this respect. Your child will be much happier and incomparably safer once he's learned to count on you. Lots of things in life are open to negotiation, but safety is not. We are not allowed to endanger our own lives or the lives of others. Only two other positive rules must be insisted upon: no child should ever be allowed to hurt another person (or any living being), nor should he be permitted to destroy property (no matter to whom it belongs). Once these three principles are established you can enjoy your child, get out of his way, and let him discover life.

Before you give any instruction, make sure you really intend to follow through: no idle threats. Use polite speech to make any request. If the child obeys, thank him pleasantly, that is verbal reinforcement. If he's slow, allow about fifteen seconds to elapse, then GET UP and make him do what you told him to do, that is gentle guidance! Don't be rough or angry, just gently positive that he WILL do what he is told to do. Thank him courteously, as though he was willing all along. NEVER tell him two or three times, just once, then ACTION!! If he's been accustomed to lots of verbal reminders and no action, it will take some time before he really believes you mean business, but don't give up.

If he throws a tantrum, gently put him in his room or, if he's under two, in his playpen, telling him he may rejoin the family when he's ready ... ready to desist from dangerous, aggressive or destructive behavior. Every boating kid (every kid of any kind) should learn this. Resist the temptation to take advantage of obedience training to control every aspect of your child's life, since he has a right to many choices.

You cannot, for example, make a child eat. When a child refuses to eat you CAN excuse him from the table and limit between meal snacks to a piece of fruit. If there is no junk food available and no big deal is made out of eating, he will soon get hungry enough to eat something. Not eating is a way children control adults, and it takes two to play that game. Don't fall for it.

Once he's learned to obey, getting the life jacket on should be simple. He should also keep his feet on the deck, his hands off the instruments, sit tight when parents are coping with emergencies, and be a pleasure to have around. Even if home has been a more casual place, the boat must not be, for the child's safety and your peace of mind.

Once you've determined that your family really enjoys the water and can accept the fact that the captain's word is law (the mate's word, also), you can start looking for a suitable cruising boat. More about that in the next chapter.

Once you've bought the safest boat you can afford, you still have to go over it from stem to stern: every inch! No one else can do it for you, it is the captain's responsibility. There are no mechanics, plumbers or firemen at sea. Once you cast off from dock or mooring you are trusting cherished lives to the seaworthiness of your craft. An ounce of prevention may well buy the lives of your children.

After making sure our previously owned boats were sound, my husband always scrubbed the whole interior with Spic and Span so I could move our babies into a sanitary environment. After that first good scrubbing, regular wash downs with a Lysol solution kept germs and mildew at bay.

Moving aboard for the season was always a red-letter day! I found really complete lists very important. Grooming, cleaning and health supplies which you regularly use at home must be aboard; skip one, and someone is miserable. It helps to stow each category of supplies together where they are most used: all cleaning supplies above or under the galley (out of reach or securely fastened), all toiletries in a handled plastic bin in the bathroom, all first aid supplies in a box near the helm (a plastic tackle box is usually adequate). A flashlight at the helm and one above your bunk help with midnight emergencies.

Every child should have his own bunk equipped with his own washable sleeping bag, an extra blanket, and a small pillow with a washable case. I have made most of these through the years, buying inexpensive yard goods and quilt batts from the Sears catalogue and utilizing worn sheets for linings and pillow cases. When the twins were born in August, 1959, I made lined beds for them from large cardboard boxes. They were safe, inexpensive and draft-free.

Every child had his own "ditty bag," made from the legs of Joe's old white Navy pants, and hung above his bunk. They all learned to pack for themselves, rolling extra jeans, shorts, sweat shirts, underwear, socks and pajamas navy-style and tucking in a favorite doll, toy and book. We never took a suitcase aboard!

Just as at home, every family member needs his own bath towel, wash cloth and toothbrush, hung separately so they can dry between usings. Even if things are different at home, cleanliness is still very important to health. Daily swimming helps keep everyone clean (if salty), but children still need a sponge bath, hair brushing and clean teeth at bedtime; cruising is no excuse for grubby children. Bedtime rituals that include friendly polishing, a storytime and extra hugs let your children know how precious they are to you.

I always use lightweight towels and washcloths for boating, they dry and stow more easily. Our collection of old swimming towels was kept separately, dried and folded in a basket under the aft coaming with the dry bathing suits. Salty things are never stowed inside. That basket, and all the bath towels, would go to a coin laundry whenever we found one. Carelessness with towels can result in impetigo. Don't let that happen.

Mosquitos and flies can constitute a real hazard to health and comfort, since boats are seldom adequately screened. Clean up right after meals and keep garbage tightly covered. Joe always helped get supper dishes done right after we finished our evening meal, while I washed the children and supervised their bedtime routines. Then we could manage with very little light until their bedtime. After we tucked the children in, Joe and I would diligently track down every mosquito, so they could sleep in peace. It still hurts me to see children covered with bites.

By the time the children were old enough for games and bridge in the evening we had a well-screened boat. We also learned that you can't win against some insect invasions, so it's best to give them the field. Our cookouts were usually staged at mid-day since early evening belongs to the mosquito. We also found some mooring areas bug-free and others simply unbearable. Before selecting a mooring site, anchor in it a few times to test for pests. Some beautiful island coves are so over-run by horse flies that they are torture for anyone, especially children who can't escape.

Childrens' fingernails should be kept short and clean so they can't scratch and infect any insect bites they do get. If the tots get into poison ivy while beach combing or berry picking, try to prevent the rash by scrubbing them with yellow laundry soap, but bring ivy lotion, just in case. Prevention is better: even little children can learn to recognize poison ivy. Jellyfish stings can be eased by applying a solution of clorox and water. Be sure to carry a sea-sickness remedy like Dramamine.

In all our years of cruising we only had one incident of sea-sickness. On that terrible day when we left Coecles Harbor in the Elco and were unmercifully pounded by the waves, Michele lost her lunch. If anyone feels queasy, a bunk down below is the worst place to go. A chair on the back deck in the open air is far better (and no bucket is needed, as long as an adult is near to hold on!)

Remain aware of your children's bowel habits while cruising. Drinking less water and getting less exercise may add up to constipation for anyone. Add more fruits and vegetables, whole grain breads and crackers and push good old water (not soda), adding some orange, lemon or grape juice and as little sugar as possible. Top this with a slice of orange and call it "vacation punch" ... you, too, can be a super salesman! Resist the temptation to bring along lots of junk food. Diets should be built around whole foods with a minimum of preservatives and chemicals. No child can reach his full potential if he subsists on snack foods.

If you have a youngster of toilet training age (18 months and up), you might find it more practical to have him use the adult toilet right from the beginning. Set him on backwards and hold him till he learns to hold on himself. It's annoying to have to carry potty seats aboard. Once kids get used to their own special "throne" they often refuse to "go," even if they desperately have to.

Keep diapers on until the training period is really over. Accidents make too much wash for boating families. Even if you don't go boating, this is sound advice. No child should have to deal with the humiliation of wet or dirty pants. If you use paper diapers, be sure to bring a few cloth diapers in case you run out. It is much easier to take a new baby boating when the mother is nursing; sincere efforts to succeed are well repaid.

No mother enjoys boating if she finds it involves endless hours in the galley, which is less convenient, spacious and equipped than its counterpart at home. The solution here lies in planning simple but nourishing favorites which can be prepared or re-heated with a minimum of equipment. Two cast-iron frying pans, a teflon coated saucepan with a tight-fitting lid, a pot big enough for the family's favorite pasta (lobster, clams, crabs, and mussels) and a whistling tea kettle are my galley slaves. I don't plan anything that needs more equipment. Foods that spatter grease are saved for cookouts.

Many meals can be planned for in-hand eating with just a napkin to save dish washing: omelet on fried toast with a banana, grilled cheese and tomato sandwich with an apple, hot dogs on rolls with raw vegetable sticks, etc. After these meals you wipe out a fry pan or two and wash some glasses. I can turn out a gourmet meal at home with pleasure, I never try to do it when I have a crowd to feed on a boat. Macaroni dishes, stew or hearty soups can be prepared at home, packed in square plastic containers in the cooler and reheated.

Everyone needs a plastic bowl for soup or cereal, a luncheon sized plate, a tupperware dessert dish, a plastic glass and a sturdy mug as well as a set of stainless flatware. Have a stash of paper plates and cups for picnics, company, rough weather, and when the water is low. I try not to use many paper goods, but there are times when they save your sanity.

Since we had so many children to feed on a limited budget, we never got into the junk food or drink habit. My food dollars are spent on real food.

Powdered milk, which might meet with substantial opposition ashore, can taste wonderful to just about anyone on a boat. Besides, the protein is the same as whole milk, and no heart of any age needs butterfat. Be sure you mix it several hours before it will be used and get it as cold as possible.

Many people associate the fun of boating with the fun of drinking. If you want to pile in the six-packs and go fishing with the boys, it's YOUR life; but I've never felt that drinking is compatible with parenting, especially under the uncommon stresses of boating. A beer or a glass of wine with dinner, or a mixed drink on special occasions are not what I call drinking. A day-long indulgence in spirits is intolerable on a boat. Anyone who is "feeling no pain" is incapable of the level of self-control, attention to detail, and reasoned response to emergency situations that family boating entails.

It is sad to see little boating orphans, stuffing themselves with junk food, vandalising property and wandering about in lonely pain while their parents "sleep it off" in crowded marinas. It is likely that alcohol is often responsible for much of the poor judgement that ends in tragedy. Drinking can also contribute to serious arguments, neglect and abuse, none of which belongs on any boat. Cruising is exciting enough!

The time together. That's what family cruising is all about. The most important signs of love are paying attention and listening. The long, slow hours on the water free your hearts and hands. You have time to really hear your children, to pay attention to them.

How I treasure the memories of the long walks on new beaches, visits to the stores in quiet towns, the browsing evening explorations in the dinghy down every creek and around every dock and mooring area.

Even if you have only one kid of your own, resist the impulse to bring another child for company. Your child shares you with a hundred other demands all year. Vacation time is better spent getting to know and relate to your own family. Besides, the responsibility for another's child on the water is more than I've ever been willing to assume, no more than I would permit my own child to go cruising in the care of another set of parents.

Bring along a few favorite books and field guides to birds and wild-flowers, as well as playing cards with extra large numbers. These permit the card games to continue even by a modest light. Always keep score, since this adds interest and improves the quality of play. Don't allow bickering or cheating, which can get out of hand and leave everyone feeling bitter. Kids need a fair referee. Bring a couple of games: monopoly and scrabble were our choices. (Herb Gliick suggested Othello, which he claims adults enjoy as much as children do.) Don't forget big pads of paper (not loose sheets), pencils and crayons (keep them out of the sun), simple fishing gear (protect fingers from hooks with little plastic covers), a clam rake, plastic bags for beach combing, and basic cookout equipment. The simplest food tastes best cooked on the beach, and the kids need lots of chance to explore and exercise.

To give me a rest, Joe often took the kids to the beach; he brought everyone who could walk, and they explored miles of shore. When I took them I usually had a baby along and/or was pregnant. Since my varicose veins were always a problem, I tried to use beach time to get off my feet. I would set up a playpen (the nylon mesh variety keeps little hands out of the sand) under an umbrella and put my low beach chair in front of it, facing the water. Then I would pace off about fifteen steps to right and left and set down my markers: sticks, stones, or a line in the sand. That would be the limits. Anyone who crossed the line would have a "time-out" (TO) on the blanket.

Except for an occasional swift rescue I could sit and bask in the sun, surrounded by busy, happy "Do-Bees." When they learned not to put everything in their mouths, the babies graduated to the sand where they gradually discovered the water. I didn't tell them not to go in too deep, children are not stupid. You can never relax vigilance, but they are almost always careful if left alone. Children whose parents are constantly cautioning them learn to manipulate their parents instead of interacting with the environment. Building complex castles and harbors, making homes for creepy-crawlies, learning to keep their footing in the shallows, watching their siblings dog-paddle and finally imitating them, they are too involved to be trying to get Mom's attention or testing fair rules.

Everyone needs a coverup shirt and a sun hat for the beach. Good tanners seldom need them but some palefaces always do. If you forget to attend to this, you can have a burned child crying all night. This is not only stupid, but cruel.

Thongs (we called them flip-flops) are also needed for the beach, in case the sand is too hot, and to go into the restroom if there is one. Traveling anywhere with kids I always carried a bathroom bag containing a can of Lysol spray, paper towels, toilet tissue and soap. I always took all the pre-school children into the ladies restroom with me. First, I cleaned the sink and toilet, then we could all safely use the facility. No one ever brought home athletes foot or anything else!

After an hour of lively play we would have a quiet time for about twenty minutes, during which everyone would lie on an individual towel, no talking allowed. Any child who was tired would drop off for a nap and I'd make some shade. When our first kids were little polio was still a dreaded possibility, so I tried to prevent fatigue. It is still a good idea.

Rest time over, we'd all have a wholesome snack before getting back to play. Once the children reached school age, I would extend exploration limits for the older children only, but I still insisted on their swimming where I could see them.

I don't know many boating families who have used their boats as much as we have. From early as possible launching to latest possible hauling, we have boarded ship every weekend and for every vacation regardless of the weather. If we could get out to the boat, we went. When the visibility was poor, the wind excessive, or the forecast gloomy, we would stay at the mooring until it improved, enjoying life afloat, nature's show and each other's company. With improving conditions we would cast off for the best adventure possible considering all circumstances. We never cancelled, just altered, our plans. I remember well that as a child I always felt so cheated when some dreamed-of outing was cancelled.

No minor illness has ever made us forego our boating. We all heal just as quickly in our seagoing home, though we have stayed closer to home at times, just in case we needed medical aid. I always carried a copy of Dr. Spock's Baby and Child Care, and a Red Cross First Aid Book, as well as confidence in myself as family medic.

Families often put off boating until their children are teenagers, but I found it most fun with little children. They conform to our schedules, while teens have a whole world of outside demands. Families who have cruised together have cemented a bond which helps them weather the inevitable growing pains. No one can ever forget all the happy times. Hard work, but definitely worth it.

Jeff, exploring on the shore of Lake Champlain

I can't end this section about taking children boating without including an excerpt from a paper our daughter, Jeanne, wrote for a composition class. Now the mother of three little daughters, Jeanne has begun to take college courses to prepare herself for a career in one of the helping professions.

THE ROCKING SEA ... by Jeanne Merkel Young

People must have thought my mother was crazy! How else can you describe a woman who takes her nine children boating every weekend? But, what other people thought never stopped my mother. So, from the time we were babies, we were rocked to sleep by the waves. We were initiated into a lifetime love of the sea.

Our excursions began with the eager packing of our duffle bags. Then, as soon as Dad returned from work on Friday, we headed for Greenport. There, we left our two cars and took the ferry to Shelter Island. It was a short walk from the ferry to Dering Harbor where our boat was moored. Hand in hand, I would walk with my father through the old village with its ginger-bread houses and sleepy streets. How I love him for those memories!

At the yacht club our dinghy awaited us. We boarded, half of us at a time, and slid out into the silent darkness, listening to the gentle lapping of the oars, watching the phosfish glow in the moonlight, drinking in the soothing salt air, thick enough to wet our hair, heady as wine.

Safe aboard, tired after our long day, we were soon tucked into our berths. Within minutes, the sea rocked us to sleep. We could barely hear our parents' murmuring voices as they planned the next day's adventures, sipping their coffee under the stars.

We would wake with the sun and, after a hearty breakfast, mother would call: "All hands on deck." My brothers would hurry to help with the mooring lines. We younger children would, literally, put our hands on the deck and laugh with joy.

Before the boat edged out of the harbor, we found a private place to enjoy the journey. The most coveted spot was the bow, where you could sit in the full force of the sea breeze and salt spray. Here, you felt the boat's power, as it swiftly cut through the waves on its way to conquer new ports. Oh, the time we had for dreaming.

Yet, we also had time for making dreams become reality. Together, we mapped out courses, called out the numbers on buoys, and spotted landmarks with our binoculars. How we fought for our turns to help.

When we reached our destination, there was the new town to explore: boatyards, little tourist shops, movie theater and, always, the ice cream parlor. With our hair brushed and on our best behavior, we'd fill two booths. Ice cream was never better.

Later, a few of us would take the dinghy and explore the nearby creeks, looking for wildlife, birds and flowers. Field guides in hand, we were always learning. Sometimes we would have a cookout and sing around a bonfire on the beach.

In the evening we played bridge by the light of a hurricane lamp. With so much practice, we all learned to play quite well by the time we were seven. There was also plenty of time for reading with no television to distract us.

Ready to give up at last, we would creep into our bunks, Mom and Dad would tuck us in and kiss us goodnight. The light would be extinguished and, again, we would be rocked to sleep in the cradle of the deep.

How beautiful our world was, how nurturing. How much a part of my soul these memories are, of the "loving seas," and the loving family. How often I regret my inability to give these same memories to my own children, since my circumstances are so different. I know the past can never be relived. I must create my own present with its own memories.

As I sit on the balcony of my small apartment overlooking Southold Bay, as I watch the boats gliding silently by, child cradled in my arms, as I recite in Spanish our favorite bedtime poem:

> "The sea, its thousands of waves, divinely rocks
> Listening to the loving seas, I rock my child and"*

I know. I know that I have given my babies a small piece of what my crazy mother gave me: a love of life, and a love of the rocking sea.

*Quote is from MECIENDO (Rocking) by Gabriella Mistral, Stanza L

Thank you, Jeanie.

11

LESSONS FROM
OUR
CRUISING LIFE

Our thirty year pilgrimage in search of the perfect boat and the perfect boat builder has taken us to boatyards from Canada to Florida. It has involved us in worry, sacrifice and expense, but these have been balanced by adventure, escape, learning, and enhanced family life.

Owning boats, (often really beyond our means), we have lived life on the high wire: perilous excitement and a few costly spills which have tested our courage and endurance. We would not exchange these years for any secure life style emphasizing the pursuit and accumulation of wealth. When deciding about life goals I have always reminded myself: "I shall not pass this way again." I believe in living my dreams.

When the cruising bug bit us we had four little children. Food, housing, clothing and doctors had first call on our earnings. As a working class family we had to limit our search to cruising boats which could be purchased for a few hundred dollars down plus three years to pay ... the American Dream. Given our income and responsibilities there was no possible way we could start with a "dream boat," but we always bought the best we could afford and improved it during our ownership.

Buying the best you can afford involves compromise and agreement. A substantial home, two good cars, and meat on the table every evening can reduce the allocation for boating. Choosing to have a smaller home, only one car, and rice and beans for supper can free money for the vacation-travel (BOAT) fund. Joe and I were lucky; we agreed on our priorities: big family, and big boat to match. Without this agreement, boat ownership can weaken family life. If one wants to go boating, rule one is: establish priorities.

If you're always dreaming about boats and wishing you could somehow get on the water, perhaps you should take the low road, especially if you have a low energy level and not much mechanical aptitude. With three or four hundred dollars you can get a fiberglass canoe or dinghy which can be carried atop your car. Every nice day you CAN go boating. You don't have to let the years slip away. Even a little boat lets you escape the crowded beaches, find a lonely rock to lie upon, drop a line over to catch flounder or mackerel, or seek out less frequented clam or mussel beds.

After being too deeply in debt for much of my own adult life, I finally have to admit that it is more prudent to determine what you can honestly afford, and look for a boat at that price.

If all you can afford is a $3,000 boat, buy the BEST boat you can find at that price. This will often result in your buying a smaller boat than you would really like, but it is the only sensible course. If you buy a 30' boat which has rotten garboards, an unreliable engine, and leaking cabins, you will NOT enjoy boating, nor will your family. You will spend time and money on frustrating repairs and layups. When you try to sell that old wreck, you will almost have to give it away. There is no increase in equity under these conditions.

It is far better to find a really sound boat for the money, even if it has to be a 16' day boat. Have patience. Get used to boating; get used to taking excellent care of that small boat. Make it a showpiece. When you get it paid for, you can turn around and sell it for a reasonable price. In the meantime, your family will be afloat in a safe, seaworthy craft which will always start (well, almost always), will be a good investment, and will not disappoint and frustrate you. Remember, good captains are trained slowly in a demanding school.

Moving up to a bigger boat should involve the same careful reasoning. Making too big a jump always ends in sorrow for the whole family. When we bought the 54' Nevins we really bit off more than we could manage. There was no way we could afford to haul, store and refurbish that large a boat, so Joe spent five futile years trying to bring it up to his high standards. When we sold it, we lost thousands of dollars. Joe's depression really began during those trying years.

If you really don't know much about boats, be sure to seek expert advice before putting your money on the line. If the boat needs work, have a reliable boatyard give you a firm estimate before you buy it.

BUILD IT YOURSELF?

Many people who want more boat than they can really afford decide to build one themselves. We have never considered that option, and think our reasoning is valid. We want a well built, quality boat; nothing else will do. Regardless of our best intentions and the excellent quality of materials we would use, there is no way, however, that we could satisfy our own standards.

Yacht design requires a professional education (five or six years); boatbuilding skills are acquired during ten or fifteen years of well-supervised work in a professional boatshop. This assumes a highly motivated individual who already has a basic knowledge of woodworking tools. This is what it takes before anyone can be judged competent to build a quality boat. Then, it takes five thousand or more hours of that highly skilled labor to build a 42' boat. We don't qualify!

Folks who try to build their dream boat while earning a living run themselves ragged for up to ten years, and end up with an inferior product. The wood dries out and, very likely, the man is not far behind. We think it is better to save and borrow to have a professionally built boat.

RESTORATION

Restoration of old boats is exciting, and we tried several times to restore lovely old ladies. If you find a sound small boat like our DOROTHY, POPOVER, or ISHMAEL, and don't plan to use it for offshore cruising, this may be a good beginning. If you have to hire the work done, be very careful. At $20 to $28 per hour (1984), boatyard bills mount unbelievably fast. Get a firm price for any planned improvement.

Alter with care. Extra weight carried too high can make a craft unseaworthy, a change in tank location or capacity can unbalance a boat, and a crude addition can destroy resale value.

For larger boats (over 34') we have sadly concluded that it is better to take the lines from worthwhile old boats and have them built from scratch. We once walked away from a 42' older boat which was selling for $16,000, only to watch its purchaser spend almost $100,000 on restoration. A couple of years later, disillusioned and much poorer, he tried to unload his folly and couldn't get $30,000. This is not a game you can win.

POWER OR SAIL?

We tortured ourselves over this qustion every time we looked for a new boat. When we had a big family to shelter, a sailboat was out of the question; we would have needed a bigger boat than we could safely have handled, considering our lack of training and experience. (We've only been sailing once, though we enjoyed it tremendously.)

As the size of our crew dwindled and we looked toward retirement, we noticed that many sailing couples switch to power as they get on in years. It gets difficult to handle big sails, though most sails can now be rigged for roller-furling. Still, finding a compatible and available crew becomes a problem. Arthritis and other health problems increase. Finally, being windswept, wet, and cold begin to lose their appeal.

We always wanted our boating season to extend from April to November, so only a powerboat with an enclosed wheelhouse or a center-cockpit motor sailer could provide enough shelter for such a long season. We were discouraged from buying a motor sailer since many of them neither sail nor motor well, though I'm sure there are notable exceptions.

We may yet give in to the temptation and try sailing, but on a very modest scale, probably nothing larger than twenty-six feet. We don't want to retire to our rocking chairs without discovering for ourselves just what is so wonderful about sailing.

As for power, no one likes to listen to engines; they are but a means. Since we must have them, safety, reliability and economy are the main considerations. On all counts, a diesel engine is superior. I would almost prefer to stay home if I had to tolerate the cantankerousness and danger of a gas engine at sea again. We have had Ford and General Motors diesels and found them both reliable and economical. I wish, however, that some company would re-issue a one-cylinder, make-or-break engine which could thump quietly along at 300 rpm; that would be real progress! My preference, then, is for inboard, diesel power, and the smallest, quietest one which will move the boat at hull speed. Frankly, I hate outboard engines and will not have one if there is any other option!

HULL TYPE

It is important to match the boat you buy to its intended use. Disregard this at your peril! Some boats are only safe in sheltered waters.

Our Steelcraft was a hard-chined plow, only safe in inland waters and on gentle rivers. We harbor-hopped along the coast with her, but took our lives in our hands on a rough sound crossing.

The Elco had a full displacement hull which was economical to operate at its hull speed of about nine knots, but it could roll your eyeballs out. With the 125 h.p. Chrysler Crown engine wide open it could go only a little faster. This boat was also safe only in protected and calm water.

The Nevins commuter yacht had a semi-displacement hull with some flare forward, but only enough for the chop on Long Island Sound. It was not adequate for offshore work. With her narrow entrance, she was usually comfortable: though she rolled, it was a soft roll. The hull speed was about eleven knots, but with two big diesels she could do over twenty knots if one was willing to buy the fuel. Her hull was beautiful!

The Egg Harbor had a round bottomed design which was supposed to offer a soft ride; with two big gas engines it could cruise at about twenty knots. At this speed, it burned up the gas but planed above any turbulence. Run at hull speed, it was at the mercy of the waves. Many "Eggs" were used as sportsfishermen by owners looking for quick trips to the fishing banks. On Long Island we called the sloppy weekend water "Chris Craft chop"; even on a windless day there were so many fast boats cris-crossing the sound that it was never calm.

Both our Uhlrichson and Zobel were lap-strake sea skiffs with semi-planing hulls, narrow entry, and enough flare to be dry. These boats are good for going fishing quite a way offshore, since they are fast and able for their size.

Our two Maine lobster type hulls were somewhat similar, since they could both cruise at about twelve knots with a single diesel engine using about five gallons per hour. We used a smaller, Ford diesel in the Fletcher boat and it was not as fast. The Fletcher boat had a box keel while the Maine boats had built down keels, which we found superior. Most Maine hulls have a good entrance, adequate flare, and enough beam to provide a stable working platform; they are economical to operate and very maneuverable. All downeast hulls are NOT equal, however, so it is absolutely necessary to have a perfected design, one which has been built successfully, so you can get a demonstration ride before placing your order. On custom-built boats costs can pile up unbelievably. If you can get a firm contract price, you'll be ahead.

We have not owned a trawler, though we have considered many of them. Originally, they were full displacement hulls, but in the last twenty years most of them have been designed with hard chine, semi-displacement hulls which deliver eight to ten knots using twin engines.

We passed a Grand Banks trawler in Buzzards Bay one day when the following sea felt like a roller coaster. Our 43' Rich boat kept ahead of the waves and we reached Onset long before the trawler. When it arrived, the skipper came by to ask who had built our boat. He'd had a rough day and could see that our Maine hull had handled the difficult sea with ease.

While the extra space in a trawler is lovely, the maintenance costs are not. A full paint job for a 42' Grand Banks can easily run to $10,000, so it helps if the owner can do some of the work himself. In any event, no wooden boat should go more than two years between paint jobs, and Joe always did our boats every year. The last time he painted the Joel White 42' boat it took him a total of 140 hours to hand-sand and paint from top to bottom. No yard would do the job that quickly or that well, I'm afraid, since most of them employ youngsters in their paint shops. Some experts estimate that you should allow ten percent of the purchase price of a wooden boat for annual maintenance, if you hire the work done.

WHY WOOD?

Wooden boat lovers don't even ask, but many other people have wondered why we always chose wooden boats instead of "easy care" fiberglass. For us, that choice is like asking whether we'd prefer a Steinway grand or a Fisher-Price plastic toy piano. There is just no comparison. A professional wants a fine instrument, others want a tough plaything. That is like comparing Tupperware to fine china. Each has its place.

It's a fact of life that many boat owners can't or won't take care of their boats; they just want to go aboard in June, shovel out the previous year's garbage, and take off. Fishermen often need a boat which asks little of them; they run their boats hard all year and come in tired at night. They would prefer to buy a new boat after ten years, rather than invest in the conscientious care of a wooden boat. Boating is not a hobby to them, it's a living.

When a boat is a home as well as a hobby, however, nothing can compare with the warmth, comfort, safety and beauty of wood. You can love a wooden boat. The big surprise is that when you start out with a well-designed, well-built wooden boat and keep up with it every season, there is actually often less work. If we could have bought a boat shed, Joe could have kept up with our 42' boat without any trouble. But then, he is not the average boat owner!

Steel and fiberglass boats have a common problem: condensation. When our four children woke up every morning on our Steelcraft, they were all wet: condensation from all that breathing. It was not as bad when it was warm and the hatch could be open, but it was unbearable in wet or cold weather (this might not be a problem for fair-weather boaters). We usually went boat hunting on foul days when Joe's work was rained out, and we found fiberglass boats dripping. Though many of them had liners of carpeting to absorb the moisture, that seemed like an unsanitary solution. Perhaps, by now, they have solved this problem. Can fiberglass be made to breathe as wood does?

Modern materials do have a place on wooden boats, however. We have had caulked plank decks and wooden hatches and found them an endless problem. We designed our Joel White boat with dynel covered plywood decks (be sure to use two layers of plywood and the proper resin) and Bomar hatches. These solutions made the ownership of a wooden boat almost trouble-free.

Opening windows are also common sources of trouble on wooden boats. We solved this problem by using Rostand opening portholes in the trunk cabin and making all wheelhouse windows fixed. They are bedded and framed with natural teak. Four-way ventilation is achieved by having three doors and an opening windshield. With the windshield and/or back door open we were usually comfortable. Our Egg Harbor had louvered aluminum windows flanking the back door, and these worked well. Sheltered by the roof overhang, they could be left open in any weather.

Many years after a fiberglass boat is scratched, faded, rusted, and mildewed, a well-cared for wooden boat will still be a "thing of beauty." Quality fiberglass boats can retain their resale value for many years, however, especially if they are maintained, and they are easier to sell since there are more people who want a sturdy toy than there are professional yachtsmen who are willing and able to care for a fine wooden boat. In spite of this practical advantage, I still find it almost impossible to be enthusiastic about owning and living on a fiberglass boat.

There is one exception: nothing beats a fiberglass dinghy! We still have the eight foot pram we bought in 1961. We paid $125 for it, second hand, and have dragged it up countless rocky beaches and tied it to impossibly rough docks. We have patched its leaks with cloth and resin several times, but this is all the care it has received. It has paid for itself many times over.

This summer, since selling our LADY JEANNE, this beat-up, little old dinghy has been our only link to the water. Tied to a tree on a lonely beach it uncomplainingly awaits our pleasure. When the sun is hot, and work ashore becomes burdensome, we pack lunch, a couple of beers, a drop-line, and our beach towels and make good our escape. The beautiful water still beckons.

SAFETY

Safety at sea is a subject which merits its own chapter, if not a whole book. I sincerely advise my readers to seek a comprehensive work including this important element. I found Charles F. Chapman's PILOTING, SEAMANSHIP and SMALL BOAT HANDLING to be very helpful. My remarks on safety are only intended to add a personal perspective.

*****

Fair weather sailors are seldom lost at sea. The few times we were in real danger were usually caused by our ignoring obvious weather signs or forecasts. Just after a hurricane is no time to begin a sea journey; the water is still too turbulent. Similarly, running in fog is dangerous and usually unnecessary, although it sometimes overtakes even cautious yachtsmen. If pressing business can't be put off, you can always leave your boat at a marina and rent a car. Don't say you can't afford this solution, since the value of even one life is incalculable.

Learn as much as possible about weather signs. Get in the habit of remembering the times of the tides and notice wind direction and velocity. Modern life has separated us from nature; life on the water tunes us in to it again. Becoming an "old salt" requires a lifetime of attention to the voices of the sea and the wind. Eric Sloan's WEATHER BOOK simplifies much weather wisdom in a way the whole family can enjoy.

I think every member of a boating family should learn to navigate. If someone is sick or disabled, the boat still has to be brought safely to port. It is surprising to realize that the compass and lead (to sound depths) were the only instruments in common use before World War II. The invention of the depth sounder was a great breakthrough. Today, navigation has become an exact science and there are wonderful instruments available at ever lower prices.

Even if you are equipped with radar and loran you should still dead-reckon your courses, however, since instruments can malfunction. This is even true if your instruments are computerized. If you punch in one wrong number, your results can be totally wrong. You have to be sure that the answers you get make sense.

With unlimited funds it is possible to make boating incredibly complicated; some engine rooms are a mind-boggling maze of wires. But, more is not always better. If you acquire equipment which you are incompetent to service or repair, you are at the mercy of technicians. I still prefer Thoreau's philosophy which, in a word, is SIMPLIFY!

In ATLANTIC HIGH, writer William F. Buckley, Jr. described steering his chartered sailing yacht with the automatic pilot from his luxurious owner's cabin. Although he had a professional crew, several radios failed to function and resisted all efforts at repair, a computer error caused a mistaken course, wet bunks were common, and the cuisine uninspired. The quality of the experience is never governed by the number, complexity and cost of the gadgets provided.

During our early years as a seagoing family, our safety was greatly augmented by taking extended cruises with another boat. If you don't have a boating friend, you might try joining a local power squadron. These organizations plan several trips each year and should have some to suit you. Some cruising clubs are too interested in excessive drinking, however, so check carefully before committing yourself.

Even with the most experienced yachtsman in the lead, all other skippers should also navigate in case the boats become separated. While monitoring channel 16 on our radio, we have often heard pitiful calls from lost sailors, many of whom did not even have their own chart, much less any real idea of their location!

Having another boat along is a life saver when some engine component fails or illness strikes. On an early cruise in the Steelcraft, the fuel pump developed a leak. We summoned friend George with a horn blast, anchored our disabled boat, and went off with him across Lake Champlain to find a new pump. Fuel pumps on old boats have twice failed us, so I would conclude that if you buy an older boat a new pump might be a sensible precaution.

We have only once had a man overboard, but because we had established good discipline it was not a dangerous occurrence. The rule that saved the day was this: there was to be no helter-skelter running from one location to another, and everyone had to be settled before we left the mooring. Then, anytime the children wanted to go forward to the bow or up to the flying bridge they had to get Joe's or my permission, and we would watch them make the journey. The same rule applied to the return trip.

The ladder to the flying bridge on our Elco went straight up the side of the wheelhouse. One day, Jeff lost his footing while climbing up. Since Joe was watching his progress he went into the water right behind Jeff. At that point Jeff was able to dog paddle but he was far from confident, so the incident could have frightened him badly. He surfaced to find himself safe in his father's arms. He opened his mouth to scream and then laughed instead. Life jackets do not eliminate the need for untiring supervision.

When the children were young, Joe and I had separate duty stations. While he was on the flying bridge with a couple of kids, I was in the aft cockpit guarding the rest of them. That was job ONE!

Chapman summarized safety at sea as "conditioned, not upon the caprice of chance or the elements, but upon the boat and the man (or woman) responsible for her." My hat is off to Joe for taking us safely through thirty years of adventure at sea. He has been a perfect captain!

KEEP A LOG

I only began to keep a log of our boat trips when the Rich boat was built. If I could begin again, I would start on the first day of the first boat. I only forgive myself by remembering that I seldom had a moment to spare during those early seafaring years. Keeping a log sharpens awareness and fosters professionalism while preserving memories and invaluable experience. Turning the pages of my logs, even years later, a descriptive entry can evoke every memorable scene.

I also wish that I had taken more pictures and that my camera had been a 35 millimeter instead of an economy model. Lack of time and money. I was too busy seeing to provisioning, safety, and comfort; accumulating a pictorial record of our adventures was not a high priority. Like a general without an orderly I had too many details to oversee, and since our budget was always strained to the limit, I could never find extra money for a better camera while I had one which still functioned.

AFTERWORD

Three months have now elapsed since we sold our lovely LADY JEANNE. Our first summer without a livaboard boat in thirty years. Have we been totally lost and miserable?

I have missed the boat, of course, but life has still been full. Once in a while when I think of Stan and Toni (the new owners) basking in the sun on the afterdeck or watching the moon rise from MY dinette, a feeling of desolation and loss creeps over me. I personally designed that boat to last for the rest of our lives and there are times when I bitterly regret being unable to keep her.

We have not wasted time on this vain regret, however, and we avoided the pain of parting by leaving for New York a few days before Stan and Toni came for the LADY JEANNE.

On that trip we stopped in Portland to see Paul and found him busy and happy. He is working as cook/waiter in a restaurant called FONE BONES where he is serious about wholesome food but otherwise quite a clown. He is also developing a musical act with some friends and trying to establish himself as a model. Someday, I know, he will find a use for his many talents.

We took a rural route through New England to Waterloo where we had a delightful few days with Jeff, Mary and little Jennifer. We had not seen this dear granddaughter since she was three months old. Now at three years of age we found her a lovely young lady. Jeff is now a fine machinist.

When we reached Long Island we went first to Sea Cliff where we spent a couple of days with my mother in my childhood home. Then, heading east, we visited Renee in Coram. April and Jessica had a new brother to show us. Trevor was born in November, but we had been too broke to take our usual trip home that fall. Such a happy boy!

On we went to Manorville for a few days with Jim. Based at his home, we visited Jeanne, Beth, Shoshana and Rivkah in Southold and Joey, Nancy, Jason, Ian and Genia in Jamesport, where Joey still runs a successful landscaping business.

Finally, the main purpose of the trip and its highlight was Jim's graduation as an electrical engineer from Stonybrook University. We joined all the Long Island children and grandchildren, plus Michele and her son Peter who flew in from Pittsburgh, and Jeff who drove from Waterloo, in cheering Jim as he accepted his hard-earned diploma. Afterward we worked together to produce a feast.

(When we go on a family visit, it can only be characterized as a pilgrimage. Elaine, in Boston, was the only child we did not see.)

Once back in Maine I set to work on this chronicle. Though much of it had already been published in WOODENBOAT and OFFSHORE, I wanted to detail several experiences and conclusions which had only been mentioned in the articles. This effort has filled all the hours between hiking, rowing, biking, fishing, berrypicking, gardening, reading and visits from five children and nine grandchildren. I have been too busy to feel sorry about having to sell the boat!

Joe has suffered more. He has always enjoyed taking care of our "ship" and, somehow, our log cabin does not take the place of a lovely yacht. How he relished his role as captain.

He has also been annoyed by the insects ashore. He never understood why folks were always complaining about the black flies in Maine. There had never been any of these infuriating creatures on the boat. Since we had always lived aboard from April to November, he had not experienced their torment. I use insect repellent, but he stubbornly swats and complains. I hope that before another black fly season arrives we will have found another boat which we can love. It must fit sensibly into our retirement budget, however, since worrying about money is not on the agenda.

During this "time out" from boating, we have settled ourselves comfortably for the last book of our lives: the growing old part. Carefully husbanded, our modest income will stretch to cover our needs. We will always find work to do, but working full time for a living is not now a goal. We have been there for too many years. While working full time, there are no hours left for just living: enjoying nature, the garden, reading, writing and sharing plans. We still have high hopes and happy dreams. Joe's depression seems to be behind him; after ten years of struggle, we know how precious health is. We spend long hours out of doors getting lots of exercise, eat only wholesome foods and very little meat, and try to avoid stress and worry. When our children entered their teens we gave up smoking, since we wanted to be a good example.

When I was a little girl I watched in wonder at the beautiful boats which filled the harbor near my Sea Cliff home. In those depression years our family couldn't even afford a row boat. I never dreamed then that I could have my own beautiful boat. Only in fairy tales could such wonders exist.

As a young family we could easily have joined the rat race seeking ever bigger homes and newer cars. How fortunate we were that our friend George's invitation to spend a day on the water brought us to a crossroad, and we took "the road less travelled."

Taking our children to sea has added incredible richness and color to our family life. In spite of all the work, worry, and expense, it has been wonderful!

During these thirty years we have been totally involved: bearing and rearing nine beautiful children and acquiring, maintaining and enjoying nine fine boats. Eighteen peak life experiences. Surely, we have been blessed.

Hearts pounding, we will still join hands and run like children down hill to every shore, our eyes hopefully scanning the harbor. One day, we will find a small ship to love again. Her fair lines will reveal the sure eye of a master designer. Like us, she will be getting on, but she'll carry herself with pride, sound of wind and limb, because her honest builder selected only fine wood and fastenings of bronze or copper. Her lovers will have known that beauty does not survive neglect; evidence of their constant attention will abound. Her cabin will be cozy and dry against all storms. No rank odor of rot or decay will foul her air.

We'll know her. Somehow, she will be ours. She will be safe in our care.

The "Footloose Friends" give Joe and Jeanne a housewarming
in their new log home.
Wade Hancock who did the cover design in background.

BIBLIOGRAPHY

AMERICAN PRACTICAL NAVIGATOR. Originally by N. Bowditch, LL.D. Washington: U. S. Hydrographic Office, 1966.

AMERICAN RED CROSS FIRST AID HANDBOOK

BIRDS OF NORTH AMERICA. Chandler S. Robbins et al. Racine, Wisconsin: Western Publishing Co., 1966.

BLUEJACKETS' MANUAL. United States Navy. Annapolis, Maryland: United States Naval Institute, 1944.

Brockman, C. Frank. TREES OF NORTH AMERICA. New York: Golden Press, 1968.

Brown, Terry and Hunter, Rob. CONCISE BOOK OF KNOTS. Agincourt: Gage Publishing, 1977.

Chapman, Charles F., PILOTING, SEAMANSHIP and SMALL BOAT HANDLING. New York: Motor Boating, 1942.

Cobb, Boughton. A FIELD GUIDE TO THE FERNS. Boston: Houghton Mifflin Company, 1963.

Duncan, Roger F., and Ware, John P., A CRUISING GUIDE TO THE NEW ENGLAND COAST. New York: Dodd, Mead & Co., 1972.

Knight, Austin M., KNIGHT'S MODERN SEAMANSHIP, New York: D. Van Nostrand Company, Inc., 1966.

Matthews, W. B., Jr., MARINE ATLAS SERIES: LONG ISLAND SOUND & SOUTH SHORE. Andover: National Book Corp., 1974.
, MARINE ATLAS SERIES: NEW ENGLAND. Andover: National Book Corp., 1977.

MERRIAM-WEBSTER DICTIONARY. Published by Pocket Books, New York, 1978. (Larger size, easy to read type.)

Morris, Percy A. A FIELD GUIDE TO SHELLS. Boston: Houghton Mifflin Company, 1973.

Murie, Olaus J. A. FIELD GUIDE TO ANIMAL TRACKS. Boston: Houghton Mifflin Company, 1974.

Peterson, Roger Tory. A FIELD GUIDE TO THE BIRDS. Boston: Houghton Mifflin Company,
, and McKenney, Margaret. A FIELD GUIDE TO WILDFLOWERS. Boston: Houghton Mifflin Company, 1968.

Pough, Richard H. AUDUBON WATER BIRD GUIDE. Garden City, New York: Doubleday & Company, 1951.

Sloan, Eric. ERIC SLOAN'S WEATHER BOOK. New York: Hawthorn Books, Inc., 1952.

Spock, Benjamin M.D. COMMONSENSE BOOK OF BABY AND CHILD CARE. New York: Duell, Sloan and Pearce, 1945.

SURVIVAL, EMERGENCY RESCUE. Department of the Air Force. Washington 25, D.C.: Air Training Command, 1962.

UNITED STATES COAST PILOT, VOL. 1., ATLANTIC COAST. National Oceanic and Atmospheric Admin., Washington, D.C.: 1978.

UNITED STATES COAST PILOT, VOL. 2., ATLANTIC COAST. National Oceanic and Atmospheric Admin., Washington, D.C.: 1978.

WATERWAY GUIDE: NORTHERN EDITION. Annapolis, Maryland: Marine Annuals, Inc., 1978.

CHARTS

12328	New York Harbor
12335	Hudson R., East R., to 67th St.
12343	Hudson R.--New York to Wappinger Creek
12347	Hudson R.--Wappinger Creek to Hudson
12348	Hudson R.--Coxsackie to Troy
14781, 2, 3, 4, 5, Champlain Canal	
14786	Erie Canal to Lake Oneida
12354	Long Island Sound--Eastern part
12358	Shelter Island Sound, Peconic Bays, Mattituck Inl.
12362	Port Jefferson and Mount Sinai Harbors
12363	Long Island Sound--Western part
12364	Long Island Sound--New Haven Harbor, Port Jefferson to Throgs Neck
12365	Long Island Sound--Oyster and Huntington Bays
12366	Long Island Sound & East River, Hempstead Harbor
12370	Housatonic River & Milford Harbor
12375, 7	Connecticut River
13205	Block Island Sound & Approaches
13214	Fishers Island Sound
13215	Block Island Sound
13219	Point Judith Harbor
13221	Narragansett Bay
13229	So. Coast of Cape Cod, Buzzards Bay
13236	Cape Cod Canal & Approaches
13246	Cape Cod Bay
13267	Massachusetts Bay, North R.
13274	Portsmouth to Boston
13275	Salem, Lynn & Manchester Harbors
13278	Portsmouth to Cape Ann
13281	Gloucester Harbor & Annisquam River
13283	Cape Neddick Hbr. to Isles of Shoals, Portsmouth Hbr.
13286	Cape Elizabeth to Portsmouth
13288	Monhegan Island to Cape Elizabeth
13290	Casco Bay
13292	Portland Harbor
13293	Damariscotta, Sheepscot & Kennebec Rivers
13296	Boothbay Harbor to Bath
13301	Muscongus Bay
13302	Penobscot Bay & Approaches
13307	Camden, Rockport & Rockland Harbors
13308	Fox Islands Thorofare
13309	Penobscot River
13312	Frenchman & Blue Hill Bays
13313	Approaches to Blue Hill Bay
13315	Deer Isle Thorofare & Casco Passage
13316	Blue Hill Bay
13318	Frenchman Bay & Mt. Desert Island
13321	Southwest Harbor & Approaches
13322	Winter Harbor

Send To . . .

LEDGE BOOKS
Box 19
Bernard, Maine 04612

Dear Reader,

    If you enjoyed NINE BOATS & NINE KIDS and would like to give a copy to a friend or relative, please use this order form for additional copies which will be sent promptly.

_____ copies, paperbound @ $9.95   total _____

_____ copies, hard cover @ $14.95   total _____

Add $1.00 postage and handling for each copy   _____

Maine residents add 5% sales tax   _____

Include your check or money order.   total _____

Name _____

Address _____

READER RESPONSE FORM

I have several other books in varying stages of readiness for publication. Will you check the titles which might interest you.

Thank you,
Jeanne St. Andre Merkel

Check
Here

_____ 1. THE BATHROOM BOOK — Help with infant care and toilet training. Discussion of everyone's bathroom problems.

_____ 2. THE HAND THAT ROCKS THE CRADLE — Sharing of experiences, ideas and inspiration from a mother of nine, grandmother of thirteen (and still counting).

_____ 3. THE OTHER MOTHER — The day care center I founded in 1966 has already cared for over 2,000 children. Founding, philosophy, model, and case studies of children.

_____ 4. WASTE NOT-- WANT NOT — A way of life. Food, clothing, shelter. Philosophy related to everyday homemaking. Practical help for everyone.